EXPERIENCING

FORGIVENESS

BY

CHARLES F. STANLEY

THOMAS NELSON
Since 1798

Published in Nashville, Tennessee, by Thomas Nelson, Inc., Publishers, and distrib-
uted in Canada by Word Communications, Ltd., Richmond, British Columbia.

Editing, layout, and design by Gregory C. Benoit Publishing, Old Mystic, CT

The Bible version used in this publication is THE NEW KING JAMES VERSION. Copyright
1979, 1980, 1982, Thomas Nelson, Inc., Publishers.

ISBN 987-1-4185-3337-3

Printed in the United States of America

08 09 10 11 12 RRD 5 4 3 2

Contents

God's Perspective on Forgiveness

Each of us has a perspective on the world and on life—a way of looking at things, of judging things, of holding things in the memory. We need to recognize that our perspective is something that we have learned, and we need to recognize that we may have adopted a wrong understanding about certain things.

I have found in my years of ministry that a wrong perspective is very common when it comes to this matter of forgiveness. Many of us have misconceptions about why God forgives us, who God forgives, what it means to be forgiven, and how we are to go about being forgiven and forgiving ourselves and others.

For the right perspective on forgiveness, we must go to God's Word and stay there. The Bible is God's foremost communication to us on this subject. It is the reference to which we must return continually to compare what *is* happening in us with what *should be* happening in us. Our perspective is wrong anytime it doesn't match up with God's eternal truth.

This book can be used by you alone or by several people in a small-group study. At various times, you will be asked to relate to the material in one of these four ways:

1. *What new insights have you gained?* Make notes about the insights that you have. You may want to record them in your Bible or in a separate journal. As you reflect back over your insights, you are likely to see how God has moved in your life.

2. *Have you ever had a similar experience?* Each of us approaches the Bible from a unique background—our own particular set of relationships and experiences. Our experiences do not make the Bible true—the Word of God is truth regardless of our opinion about it. It is important, however, to share our experiences in order to see how God's truth can be applied to human lives.

3. *How do you feel about the material presented?* Emotional responses do not give validity to the Scriptures, nor should we trust our emotions as a gauge for our faith. In small-group Bible study, however, it is good for participants to express their emotions. The Holy Spirit often communicates with us through this unspoken language.

4. *In what way do you feel challenged to respond or to act?* God's Word may cause you to feel inspired or challenged to change something in your life. Take the challenge seriously and find ways of acting upon it. If God reveals to you a particular need that He wants you to address, take that as "marching orders" from God. God is expecting you to do something with the challenge that He has just given you.

Start and conclude your Bible study sessions in prayer. Ask God to give you spiritual eyes to see and spiritual ears to hear. As you conclude your study, ask the Lord to seal what you have learned so that you will never forget it. Ask Him to help you grow into the fullness of the stature of Christ Jesus.

Again, I caution you to keep the Bible at the center of your study. A genuine Bible study stays focused on God's Word and promotes a growing faith and a closer walk with the Holy Spirit in each person who participates.

Lesson 1

Experiencing Complete Forgiveness

─── &. **In This Lesson** ɕ ───

LEARNING: WHAT EXACTLY IS FORGIVENESS?

GROWING: HOW CAN I STOP BEING AN UNFORGIVEN PERSON?

"Forgive me? How could God ever forgive me? You don't know what I've done." "Forgive that person after what she did to me? You've got to be kidding!" "I can't believe I've done such an awful thing. I can never forgive myself for doing that."

These are confessions that I have heard often as a pastor. They are the confessions of people who have godly parents, who have grown up in church, and who have heard sermons about forgiveness all their lives, yet they persist in believing that there is something unique about their situation that puts them beyond God's forgiveness.

The result is bondage. The bondage of living in guilt and unforgiveness stifles a person's ability to love and to receive love. It stunts the growth of marriages and friendships. It keeps a person from entering into all that the Lord might have for him in the way of ministry or outreach. It keeps a person from enjoying the full abundant life that Christ promised to those who believe in Him (John 10:10). And bondage, my friend, is never the desire of God for His children.

God's desire for you today is that you be free in your spirit—free to embrace all the blessings, challenges, and joys that the Lord has for you now and in your future. God's desire is for you to experience *complete* forgiveness, which is forgiveness of your sins and a full restoration in your relationship to the Lord God, forgiveness of others who have wronged you, and forgiveness of yourself.

Limited forgiveness will never do. Complete forgiveness is required if you are to know personally and fully that God is your loving heavenly Father, and if you are ever to reach your personal destiny in this life.

A Definition of Forgiveness

At the outset of this Bible study we must define forgiveness.

Forgiveness does not mean, "It didn't matter." If you have been hurt by someone, or if you have committed a sin, it does matter. There is no justification for sin that stands up in God's presence. If you have sinned, you need to recognize that your sin is a blot on your soul, one that you can't and therefore shouldn't attempt to sweep under the rug or ignore. Sin matters. Hurt, pain, bondage, and guilt come in the aftermath of sin, and you are unwise to deny their reality.

Forgiveness does not mean, "I'll get over it in time." The memory of a particular incident or action may fade with time, but it never disappears. If you have committed a sin before God, the effects of that sin remain in your life until you receive God's forgiveness for it. You may not immediately feel the consequences of your sin—which can cause you to think that God has overlooked your sin or that it has been resolved in some way—but the consequences of sin will manifest themselves. They lie as dormant "bad seeds" in your life.

The same holds true for a wrong that another person commits against you. You may think that time will heal. Time by itself doesn't heal anything. Only the Lord Jesus Christ and His forgiveness working in and through you can heal the hurt that you have felt. A wrong that you attempt to bury will only rot in your heart and very easily can turn into bitterness, anger, and hatred—all of which are destructive emotions to the person who harbors them, as well as the root of destructive behavior that may affect others.

Forgiveness does not mean, "There will be no penalty." Some people believe that God skips over certain sins when He surveys the hearts of people. This is usually the response of people who *hope* that God will make a detour around their sin and that they'll get away with it.

There are other times, however, when we are fearful that God will forget to punish those who have wronged us. They may even seem to be prospering, and we feel a need to hold on to our unforgiveness until we are certain that the other people are punished in some way. We hold on to the prerogative of vengeance just in case God has forgotten about the incident or in case He intends to do nothing about it. At other times, we know that we deserve to be punished, but God doesn't seem to be taking any negative action against us, so we refuse to forgive ourselves as a form of self-punishment.

These definitions don't hold water when they are subjected to the truth of God's Word. Sin matters. It *always* matters. Sin and the effects of sin don't disappear over time of their own natural accord. Sin must be forgiven, or it remains unforgiven. Sin *always* has consequences. It always bears with it the ultimate penalty of death.

What then is forgiveness? *Forgiveness* is the act of setting someone free from an obligation to you that is a result of a wrong done against you. It involves three elements:

5

1. An injury. A wrong is committed. Pain, hurt, suffering, or guilt is experienced (consciously or subconsciously).

2. A debt resulting from the injury. There is a consequence that is always detrimental and puts someone into a deficit state of some kind.

3. A cancellation of the debt.

We'll be looking at each of these elements in greater depth in this study. All three elements are involved in forgiveness of all types—forgiveness by God, forgiveness of others, and forgiveness of self.

Unforgiven People

People who haven't received God's forgiveness are in pain. There is a festering wound in the soul. There is a wall in the spirit that keeps them imprisoned. They may not recognize that they are in a state of unforgiveness, but many people who feel frustrated, burdened, impatient, angry, jealous, or bitter are victims of unforgiveness.

Forgiveness brings *freedom*. It brings with it the manifestation of the fruit of the Spirit: love, joy, peace, patience, kindness, goodness, faithfulness, gentleness, self-control (Gal. 5:22–23). Forgiveness is God's desire for you. Therefore, in this series of Bible study lessons we'll explore what it means to be forgiven, and what we need to do to experience God's complete forgiveness in our lives.

⚘ When you hear the word unforgiven, is there someone who comes to mind immediately (perhaps even yourself)?

⚘ When have you struggled with issues of forgiveness and un-forgiveness? Have you experienced God's forgiveness in your life? Have you experienced forgiveness from someone else?

⚘ How does it feel to be forgiven? How does it feel to be unfor-given?

> Do you not know that the unrighteous will not inherit the
> kingdom of God? Do not be deceived. Neither fornicators, nor
> idolaters, nor adulterers, nor homosexuals, nor sodomites, nor
> thieves, nor covetous, nor drunkards, nor revilers, nor extor-
> tioners will inherit the kingdom of God. And such were some
> of you. But you were washed, but you were sanctified, but you
> were justified in the name of the Lord Jesus and by the Spirit
> of our God.
>
> —1 Corinthians 6:9–11

This passage holds three great messages for us.

First, it tells us that sin is sin. God doesn't differentiate between one
type or brand of sin and another. Most of us wouldn't think of revilers
(slanderers) as being in the same category as thieves, but God doesn't
have categories of sin. Sin is sin.

Later in the same chapter, Paul made a distinction between the sin of
sexual immorality and other sins, teaching the Corinthians that "every
sin that a man does is outside the body, but he who commits sexual
immorality sins against his own body" (1 Cor. 6:18). But this is a dif-
ferentiation of sin according to the effects of certain sinful behaviors,
not the nature of sin itself.

Second, it tells us that sin is a lifestyle, a mind-set, a state of being. Paul
was not condemning one specific act or behavior; rather, he was stating
that sin had been the identity of the Corinthians in the past. Sin had
been their all-consuming character. For example, he didn't say, "Some
of you have taken things that weren't yours." Paul called them former
thieves—people who had stolen as a way of life. He didn't say, "Some of
you had one too many drinks on occasion." He said some in the Corin-
thian church were *drunkards*.

Now before you start thinking, "Well, I haven't been any of the things on Paul's list," let me quickly advise you that this is not a definitive list. Paul wasn't trying to list all types of sinners. Rather, he was giving examples of the sinful state to point out the same truth that he shared with the Romans: "All have sinned and fall short of the glory of God" (Rom. 3:23). Every person, before receiving a new identity in Christ Jesus, has had the identity of a sinner.

Some people look back over their lives and conclude, "I've never done anything very bad. I'm a pretty good person and always have been." And sometimes they conclude, "What is there that God needs to forgive?" They have missed the entire point about sin and forgiveness. They have been taught a wrong perspective on life and on themselves. This is the perspective that the Romans apparently had, for Paul spent much of the book of Romans teaching that we are born with a sin nature.

Sin isn't something that you *do*. Rather, being sinful is something that you *are* from birth.

Third, this passage tells us that all types of sin can be forgiven. Paul said, "And such *were* some of you" (v. 11, emphasis added). Then Paul reminded them that they were no longer who they were, but they had been washed, sanctified, and justified in the name of the Lord Jesus and by the Spirit of God. The Corinthians found a new life, a new identity in Christ Jesus!

Note the words that Paul used:

⮞ *Washed.* Paul spoke of a cleansing of the spirit. So did the psalmist when he said, "Purge me with hyssop, and I shall be clean; wash me, and I shall be whiter than snow" (Ps. 51:7).

Sanctified. Something that is sanctified is dedicated to God, set aside for holy uses. In Old Testament times, blood from sacrificed animals was applied to certain vessels in the tabernacle to make them holy for God's use. Hebrews 13:12 states, "Therefore Jesus also, that He might sanctify the people with His own blood, suffered." When God forgives us, He sets us aside—apart from the world of unredeemed, unregenerate, unforgiven mankind—and considers us to be solely for His purposes and fellowship.

Justified. When we justify something, we line it up—for example, we justify the margins on a page or we justify our legal arguments against the law of the land. When we are justified in our actions, we are vindicated. In forgiveness, God lines us up against the truth of what Jesus did on the cross, and God vindicates us and declares us to be righteous just because we are lined up with Jesus. We aren't righteous in ourselves, but the shed blood of Jesus justifies us before God.

Nothing is beyond God's forgiveness. No sin is too great, too awful, or too prolific for God to forgive. No person is so deep in sin, so ingrained in a lifestyle, so steeped in evil, that he cannot be saved.

Use the table on the next page to identify who you were before you received Jesus as Savior, and who you are now.

I once was . . .	But now I'm . . .

The Nature of Sin

In the introduction, I defined *forgiveness* as "the act of setting some-one free." *Sin*, by contrast, is "the state of being in bondage—in need of being set free." This state is described in Psalm 51 as the result of transgressions, iniquity, sin, and evil.

We do what we do because we are sinners. Our sinful actions seal the fact that we are sinners. Our being and doing are cyclical. We may not always admit to being sinners, but deep down inside, we recognize that we are sinners, and we have an awareness that we have sinned or are sinning.

The sinner knows at some level that he is sinning. Sin involves the will, and it also affects the memory—we remember our sins. They don't just float by unnoticed or ignored. The psalmist is very open about this: "For I acknowledge my transgressions, and my sin is always before me" (Ps. 51:3).

How do we know that we are sinners or that we have sinned? God built into each one of us an alarm system called the conscience. It sounds each time we do something, or are about to do something, that we know is wrong. If we ignore the alarm system, our sensitivity to evil becomes dull, and eventually we stop hearing the alarm. Be very concerned if you *never* hear that still small voice inside you saying, "This is wrong and you know it." A healthy conscience is something to cherish and to nurture.

The flaw in the conscience, however, is that it is based on human understanding of what is right and wrong. The difference between right and wrong is something that we learn. Unfortunately, some people are taught that right is wrong and wrong is right. They make decisions and behave in ways that are sinful with little remorse—that is, until they are confronted with the truth.

The conscience always is pricked to some degree in the presence of the pure expression of the gospel of our Lord Jesus Christ. Jesus Christ is "the way, the truth, and the life" (John 14:6). He stands in sharp contrast to all that leads to destruction; He opposes all that is a lie or that contributes to death. In the presence of the gospel, even the most warped conscience is confronted with God's absolutes.

The best thing you can instill in your children is the knowledge of the gospel of God's Word. The best thing you can do to keep your conscience alive is to steep it in the Word of God. If you were taught a faulty perspective of right and wrong, read God's Word without ceasing in order to bring about a transformation in your mind.

But you were washed, but you were sanctified, but you were justified in the name of the Lord Jesus and by the Spirit of our God.

—1 Corinthians 6:11

❧ Give definitions in your own words for each of the following:

Washed:

Sanctified:

Justified:

❧ How does each of these things affect your sinful nature? Your specific, individual sins?

15

Believers in Christ Jesus have a dual alarm system. We have the natural conscience that has been given to every person, and we also have the Holy Spirit indwelling us. The Holy Spirit provides strong counsel that we are acting, or are about to act, in a way that is contrary to God's desire. The Holy Spirit always points us toward Jesus and to the fullness of the Word of God. Jesus called the Holy Spirit the "Spirit of truth," our divine counselor (John 14:15–17; 15:26).

The Holy Spirit will never quit speaking to you once you have received Him into your life. Your spiritual ears may become dull, but you can never completely silence the Holy Spirit. If you don't feel the Holy Spirit pricking your heart from time to time, you may need to ask, "Am I really saved? Have I really received forgiveness from God for my sinful state?"

Listen to your conscience and to the Holy Spirit today. He will tell you whether you are in need of forgiveness.

> If you love Me, keep My commandments. And I will pray the Father, and He will give you another Helper, that He may abide with you forever—the Spirit of truth, whom the world cannot receive, because it neither sees Him nor knows Him; but you know Him, for He dwells with you and will be in you.
>
> —John 14:15–17

∼ List below the specific names and qualities of the Holy Spirit found in these verses.

෴ What exactly does the Holy Spirit do? What are *we* expected to do, according to these verses?

What About the Unpardonable Sin?

Let's take a close look at the passage of Scripture that describes the unpardonable sin. In Matthew 12, Jesus and His disciples pluck and eat some heads of grain as they pass through a field. Then, while in a synagogue, He heals a man with a withered hand. Jesus does these things on the Sabbath, and the Pharisees speak out against Him and begin to plot to destroy Him. (See vv. 1–13.) Jesus knows what they are up to.

Then Jesus heals a person who is demon-possessed and cannot see or speak. There can be no doubt that this man has been healed in a powerful way. The Pharisees, intent solely on destroying any credibility that Jesus might have with the people, insist that He has healed by the power of Beelzebub, the ruler of the demons. Jesus replies, "Every kingdom divided against itself is brought to desolation" (Matt. 12:25). In other words, Satan isn't going to empower or inspire anybody to do something that is good. Satan would be setting up his own downfall.

The Pharisees are also claiming that God would not empower someone like Jesus to do good on the Sabbath. They are saying, in essence, "God is content to let certain people starve or suffer on the Sabbath, but the ruler of the demons, Beelzebub, is willing to see such people helped and healed." What a complete perversion of the truth about God's nature, and also about the devil's nature!

17

Jesus states, "He who is not with Me is against Me, and he who does not gather with Me scatters abroad" (Matt. 12:30). Then He says these words, which are considered the definition of the unpardonable sin:

> Therefore I say to you, every sin and blasphemy will be forgiven men, but the blasphemy against the Spirit will not be forgiven men. Anyone who speaks a word against the Son of Man, it will be forgiven him; but whoever speaks against the Holy Spirit, it will not be forgiven him, either in this age or in the age to come.
>
> —Matthew 12:31–32

Jesus is saying, "You can say what you will about me, but don't speak such perversion about the Spirit of God. When you blaspheme against God in that way, you are saying that God does not desire to forgive and deliver people. As long as you believe that and teach that to others, you won't be able to experience His forgiveness and deliverance. If you don't believe that God wants to forgive people and restore them to wholeness, then you will never be open to the sacrifice that I will make on the cross of Calvary."

These words of Jesus were to the Pharisees, people who had put themselves into sharp conflict with Jesus and who were plotting His destruction. He was speaking to them before His death on the cross and before His resurrection. These words were spoken as a warning to the Pharisees to let them know that He knew the full intent of their hearts and the full meaning of their claims.

Jesus says immediately after this warning, "Either make the tree good and its fruit good, or else make the tree bad and its fruit bad; for a tree is known by its fruit. Brood of vipers! How can you, being evil, speak good things?" (Matt. 12:33–34). Jesus is saying, "Either make Me good and of a good God, or make Me bad and call God bad. Judge what I do. Is it good or bad? I'm willing to do that regarding you. I call you a brood of snakes. And since you are evil, I say plainly that there is no way that anything you say can be good."

The unpardonable sin is the sin of the Pharisees, committed before the Cross. It is not a sin that you need to be concerned about today. If you have any concern about having committed the unpardonable sin—any concern that you might not be right with God, even though you hope and desire to be right with God—you have not committed the unpardonable sin!

Let me point out two other facts based on God's Word:

First, there is no exception clause in any of the Scriptures that offer salvation. John 3:16 does *not* say, "For God so loved the world—except those who have committed a certain type of sin—that He gave His only begotten Son, that whoever—except those who are sinners of a particular brand—should not perish but have everlasting life."

Romans 6:23 does *not* say, "The gift of God is eternal life in Christ Jesus our Lord—except to one particular category of sinners."

First John 1:9 does *not* say, "If we confess our sins, He is faithful and just to forgive us our sins and to cleanse us from all unrighteousness—except in the specific case of [fill in the blank]." No! God's call to salvation is a call to all sinners.

Second, there is no warning in the Gospels or in the Epistles about an unpardonable sin. Paul, Peter, John, and the other writers of the New Testament did not say to us, "Watch out for this one sin. God can forgive all sins but that one." No! There is no sin that is unforgivable on this side of the grave.

If we say that we have no sin, we deceive ourselves, and the truth is not in us. If we confess our sins, He is faithful and just to forgive us our sins and to cleanse us from all unrighteousness.

—1 John 1:8–9

❧ According to these verses, what is required to receive forgiveness of sins?

❧ What is the only condition where a person does *not* receive forgiveness, according to these verses?

An Unpardonable State

The sin that grieves the Holy Spirit and can quench the work of the Spirit in your life is a refusal to receive the forgiveness that God freely offers to you. You can refuse God's offer of forgiveness to the point that you have a hardened heart. You can become calcified to the gospel over time. And that creates an *unpardonable state*.

God will not reach beyond the boundaries of your own free will and save you against your will! You can die in an unpardonable state, but it won't be because you have committed an unpardonable sin. As I stated above, no sin is unforgivable on this side of death. It is equally true that no sin can be forgiven on the other side of the grave.

The only thing that can keep people from being forgiven is the refusal to *accept and receive* what Jesus Christ has done for them on the cross. Refusing to accept the forgiveness made available by the death of Christ brings about everlasting death. Accepting what Jesus did on the cross—believing in Him as Savior—brings about everlasting life.

Forgiveness Must Only Be Received

Have you made a decision to accept and receive Jesus as your personal Savior? To "accept and receive"—that's all that's required for you to be forgiven by God, regardless of the nature, magnitude, or deep entrenchment of your sins.

To "accept" is to believe with your mind what the Bible says about Jesus and His death on the cross: that Jesus died for your sins, and that He rose to give you new life in Him. To "receive" is to say, "I don't merely accept what Jesus did on the cross as a fact of history, but I accept His sacrificial death for me personally—the sacrifice that was made for my sins. I invite the Holy Spirit to indwell me, to cleanse me of all my past sin, and to make me a new person in God's eyes. I receive the work of the Holy Spirit in me that gives me a completely restored relationship with my heavenly Father."

God desires to forgive you today. Have you taken Him up on His offer? If not, will you accept and receive Jesus Christ today? Will you receive God's forgiveness?

Not by works of righteousness which we have done, but according to His mercy He saved us, through the washing of regeneration and renewing of the Holy Spirit.

—Titus 3:5

❧ What are "works of righteousness"? Why can such things never wash away sin?

❧ What is the "washing of regeneration"? What is involved in that process?

❧ What is *my* part in "regeneration" and "renewing"? What is the Holy Spirit's part?

Today and Tomorrow

TODAY: THE ONLY UNPARDONABLE SIN IS REJECTING JESUS' FREE OFFER OF SALVATION.

TOMORROW: I WILL YIELD MYSELF TO THE HOLY SPIRIT, CONFESSING SINS QUICKLY.

Notes and Prayer Requests:

LESSON 3

The Foundation for Our Forgiveness

❧ In This Lesson ☙

LEARNING: IF SIN IS SO AWFUL, WHY DOES GOD FORGIVE IT?

GROWING: WHAT IS MY ROLE IN FINDING FORGIVENESS?

Why does God forgive people? Many people think that God *has* to forgive people for this reason or that. God doesn't *have* to do anything! God certainly doesn't forgive us for any of these reasons:

He doesn't forgive us because we are good people. We all know that we *aren't* good. Even Jesus said, "No one is good but One, that is, God" (Matt. 19:17). We live in a fallen world, and we are born in a fallen state. The apostle Paul wrote:

> Therefore, just as through one man sin entered the world, and death through sin, and thus death spread to all men, because all sinned.... Nevertheless death reigned from Adam ... even over those who had not sinned according to the likeness of the transgression of Adam, who is a type of Him who was to come.
>
> —Romans 5:12–14

Like it or not, we are Adam's heirs. We are born in a sinful state, separated from God and in need of God's forgiveness and reconciliation to Himself.

He doesn't forgive us because we promise never to sin again. In all probability, we will sin again, and God knows it even if we won't admit it to ourselves.

He doesn't forgive us because we go to church or give money to worthy causes. Our works, as noble as they may be, have nothing to do with our salvation. We see this clearly in Ephesians 2:8–9: "For by grace you have been saved through faith, and that not of yourselves; it is the gift of God, not of works, lest anyone should boast."

He doesn't forgive us because He is having a good day and feels kindly toward mankind. God is not capricious, bestowing forgiveness on one day and withholding it on the next. God's nature doesn't change; He isn't ruled by whim; He doesn't operate according to an emotional barometer. When things go well, some people comment, "God was smiling on me today." The fact is, God is always smiling on us.

He doesn't forgive us because we ask Him to forgive us. God forgives us *when* we ask Him to forgive us, but He doesn't forgive us *because* we ask Him. That would imply that God is in a state of unforgiveness toward us until we ask, which simply isn't the case. God is always extending an offer of forgiveness to us. Our plea for forgiveness doesn't move God to action; He has already moved toward us—all the way from heaven right to the place where we live in our sin—and He is waiting for us to turn to Him and receive the forgiveness that He offers.

He doesn't forgive us because He is a good God and would never send anybody to hell. That's one of the foremost heresies of our time. I hear it often: "God is a good God, and He'd never condemn a person to an eternity without Him." That isn't what the Bible teaches. John 3:16 is followed by these words:

> For God did not send His Son into the world to condemn the world, but that the world through Him might be saved. He who believes in Him is not condemned; but he who does not believe is condemned already, because he has not believed in the name of the only begotten Son of God. And this is the condemnation, that the light has come into the world, and men loved darkness rather than light, because their deeds were evil.
>
> —John 3:17–19

Our actions condemn us. God doesn't desire that any should perish, but He will not override our will. If someone chooses to reject God's offer of forgiveness, then he has chosen his eternal destiny without God.

🖎 According to John 3:17–19 (above), what prevents people from accepting God's gift of salvation?

🖎 According to those verses, why does God forgive?

🖎 According to those verses, what is the result of rejecting Jesus' salvation?

26

What Motivates God to Forgive?

The motivation for God's forgiveness lies totally within God Himself. He forgives us because He wants to forgive. God forgives out of His unconditional, eternal love. John tells us that God's very nature is love, and forgiveness flows from His nature (1 John 4:8–10). We are forgiven because it is God's will to forgive.

> But God, who is rich in mercy, because of His great love with which He loved us, even when we were dead in trespasses, made us alive together with Christ (by grace you have been saved).
>
> —Ephesians 2:4-5

✎ According to these verses, why does God forgive?

✎ According to these verses, what happens when we receive Christ as our Savior?

God Sets the Rules for Forgiveness

Forgiveness is totally at God's initiative and subject to God's will alone, so we must ask, "Has God established any rules or protocol for forgiveness?" He certainly has.

We must recognize that God is holy, which means that He is separate from mankind in nature. God has no capacity for sin, and He cannot have fellowship with sin. God is totally pure, righteous, and without fault. He cannot coexist where sin is present.

Light and dark do not exist simultaneously. In a similar manner, your sin cannot exist in God's presence. God obliterates sin just as light obliterates darkness, and in that we find a picture of our vulnerability before God when we are filled with sin. We are subject to being consumed by Him as darkness is consumed by light, having the innermost being vaporized by His fire of righteousness. In a word, we are subject to death.

God made a provision, however, for us to be cleansed of sin so that we might have fellowship with Him—that provision was in the form of a blood sacrifice. "But I don't like this idea of blood," you may say. The idea of blood sacrifice was not our idea—it was God's idea. It is not within our prerogative to choose another means for reconciliation with God. God sets the rules in this matter, and God established the blood sacrifice as a means of reconciling us to Him.

There is no forgiveness without blood sacrifice. This theme is in the Bible from cover to cover. When Cain and Abel made sacrificial offerings to God, the offering that was accepted by God was the blood sacrifice of a lamb. (See Gen. 4:2–5.)

The sacrifices that atoned for sin under the law of Moses were blood sacrifices. In like manner, the blood of Jesus shed on the cross of Calvary is the *sacrificial, substitutionary, all-sufficient atonement* for our sins. Each of the words in the previous sentence is important to our understanding of the forgiveness made available to us through the death of Jesus Christ.

‾ **Sacrificial.** Jesus gave His life on the cross as a sacrifice. He wasn't put to death by the Romans or the Jewish leaders. On the contrary, Jesus appeared in history to "put away sin by the sacrifice of Himself" (Heb. 9:26). Jesus gave His life, as an act of His will conforming to the Father's will, as the "Lamb slain from the foundation of the world" (Rev. 13:8).

‾ **Substitutionary.** Jesus took your place on the cross. He died in your place and in my place, and in the place of everyone that you know. The penalty for sin is death. And we are all sinners. Unless One who was pure and righteous took our place and suffered the penalty for our sin, we would have to bear that penalty ourselves. The apostle Paul explained this by citing several verses from the Old Testament:

There is none righteous, no, not one;
There is none who understands;
There is none who seeks after God.
They have all turned aside;
They have together become unprofitable;
There is none who does good, no, not one.
Their throat is an open tomb;
With their tongues they have practiced deceit;
The poison of asps is under their lips;
Whose mouth is full of cursing and bitterness.

> Their feet are swift to shed blood;
> Destruction and misery are in their ways;
> And the way of peace they have not known.
> There is no fear of God before their eyes.

> —Romans 3:10–18

~ *All-sufficient*. The work that Jesus did was definitive. We no longer need to offer blood sacrifices in acknowledgment of our sin. We only need to have faith in Jesus Christ and to accept what He has done on our behalf. The writer of Hebrews says that God took away the first means of blood sacrifice that He might establish the second means, the sacrifice of Jesus. The sacrifice of Jesus was the only one necessary. The phrase that is used is a powerful one: "once for all" (Heb. 10:10).

~ *Atonement*. *Atonement* means "reconciliation"—"at-one-ment". Jesus' death on the cross made it possible for the gap to be bridged between God and people. Romans 5:1 speaks of atonement in terms of peace: "Therefore, having been justified by faith, we have peace with God through our Lord Jesus Christ."

What Jesus did on the cross, He never needs to do again, and neither does anyone else ever have to suffer and die as He did. He is the sacrificial, substitutionary, all-sufficient atonement.

> For the death that He died, He died to sin once for all; but the life that He lives, He lives to God. Likewise you also, reckon yourselves to be dead indeed to sin, but alive to God in Christ Jesus our Lord.

> —Romans 6:10-11

What does it mean to be "dead to sin"? How do we balance this with the fact that Christians still commit sin?

Why does Paul tell us to "reckon ourselves" (or think of ourselves) as being dead to sin? What does our thinking have to do with the process?

Jesus: Example or Sacrifice?

Some people believe that Jesus came to be our example of how to live a good life. To be sure, Jesus is our example of righteousness. We are to grow up into His nature and become like Him, but that isn't the reason that Jesus came. Jesus came to die. His purpose was to be the sacrificial, substitutionary, all-sufficient atonement. If Jesus didn't come for this reason, why did Jesus die? What purpose would His death have if not for forgiveness?

Jesus could have spared His own life. His power to calm a raging sea, to heal and deliver, is evidence of His ability to summon the forces of heaven on His behalf. His quick thinking and speaking in outwitting

31

the scribes and Pharisees are evidence that He could have argued His case favorably before Pilate. If Jesus had insisted on His natural human will in the matter, He could have walked away from Gethsemane, walked away from Jerusalem, and walked away from the Cross long before His arrest in the Garden. But He submitted His will to that of His heavenly Father, saying, "Not as I will, but as You will" (Matt. 26:39).

If Jesus didn't come to die, there is no purpose in the Cross or the Resurrection that followed. Some say that Jesus was sacrificed as a ransom to buy off the devil. But Scripture offers no evidence for that. Others say that Jesus died a holy, righteous man as a bitter example to us that sin is awful and destructive—to the point that we kill the best and the brightest. But such reasoning violates every principle of salvation, softens the death consequence of sin, and belittles the holiness of God. It is an idea deeply rooted in humanistic religion.

Again and again in the New Testament we are confronted with the message: Christ died for us. Jesus came so that you and I might transfer our guilt to Him, and accept, by faith, that He is the guiltless One who has received our sin and taken it on Himself. If you are looking for forgiveness on the basis of your pleas, promises, and performance, you will remain in sin and guilt. If you accept His sacrifice on your behalf, you will receive the fullness of God's life-giving Spirit.

> My little children, these things I write to you, so that you may not sin. And if anyone sins, we have an Advocate with the Father, Jesus Christ the righteous.
>
> —1 John 2:1

🖎 Why does John say "so that you may not sin," then immediately speak about times when we *do* sin?

🖎 What is an "advocate"? What sort of advocate is Jesus?

🖎 Today and Tomorrow 🖎

TODAY: GOD HAS FORGIVEN ME BECAUSE HE *WANTED* TO—IT'S THAT SIMPLE.

TOMORROW: I WILL REFLECT UPON WHAT MY FREE SALVATION COST GOD.

33

Lesson 4

A Matter of Life and Death

---------------- ❧ **In This Lesson** ❦ ----------------

Learning: What exactly is sin?

Growing: Why do I need forgiveness in the first place?

Forgiveness is a matter of life and death—eternal life and death. There isn't anything more important than to receive God's forgiveness and be reconciled to Him. In the last lesson, I introduced several concepts about sin and forgiveness. I want to build on them in this lesson and take you into a fuller understanding of what the Bible teaches about sin, guilt, and our need for a Savior.

You may be a Christian and therefore believe that you don't need to know anything more about sin and guilt. Well, as a Christian, you should be talking to people who are sinners about their need for forgiveness. This lesson can give you some insights into what to say about sin and forgiveness, and how to encourage a person to accept Christ as Savior.

True or False Guilt

Let's recognize several facts about guilt. First, genuine guilt is the way that we feel when we have sinned. It is the normal response to sinful behavior. Sin causes guilt, but not all guilt comes from sin. The guilt that we feel is sometimes false guilt.

Consider for a moment the young woman who is a victim of incest or rape. She may struggle for years with a sense of guilt because she has been a party to a sin. But she was neither the initiator of nor a willing participant in that sin. She is a victim of someone else's sin. The guilt that she feels is false guilt. It is false because, from God's perspective, there is no accountability placed upon the other person for what happened. True guilt is associated with willful sin, not sin that is against one's will.

An Accountability Ladder Involving the Will

Genuine guilt arises when we willfully act in a way that we know is contrary to God's law. An accountability ladder involving the will looks something like this:

forgiveness
sin and guilt
knowledge
moral conscience

Forgiveness presupposes sin and its attendant guilt. In other words, if you feel no guilt of sin, you feel no need for forgiveness. Guilt presupposes knowledge. If you don't know that you have sinned, you don't feel guilty. Knowledge presupposes a moral conscience—that you have the capacity for determining right from wrong. If you don't have a moral conscience, you don't know whether you are doing wrong. If you are unable to determine right from wrong—perhaps because you are mentally disabled—then you cannot be held accountable for your actions.

In this entire chain of presuppositions is the concept of the will. Put the process in reverse: If you have the capacity to know right from wrong, and you know that something is wrong but you do it anyway, you will feel guilty and have a need for forgiveness. You have acted out of your will to do something that you know not to do. You have willfully acted in a way that is wrong, and you are accountable for your actions.

You may say, "Are you telling me that if I don't know that something is wrong, I'm not accountable for that sin?" That's exactly what I'm saying, but hear me carefully when I say that very few people fall into that category. Most of us know what to do. Most of us know what not to do. And most of us choose, at some points in our lives, to do what we know not to do. This is true for all people. Human beings around the world have an intuitive sense of what is right and wrong, and they know when they are choosing wrong.

Consider for a moment a three-year-old child who is told specifically, "Don't touch Mommy's special vase." The child is brought into the living room and told, "In this room, I want you to look at things but not touch them." The child may even be shown the vase and be allowed to touch it under careful supervision while her mother says, "This is the vase I don't want you to touch, except when I am with you and we are touching it just as we are touching it right now."

The mother asks the child, "Do you understand what I am telling you?" The child nods yes and may even say, "I won't touch your vase, Mommy." The next hour, what does Mommy hear from the living room? The crash of her favorite vase.

Now, nobody had to teach that little girl to disobey. We teach our children to obey, but they are born with the ability to disobey. Even when we know that we aren't to do certain things because God has commanded us not to do them, we sometimes still choose to do those things. Paul wrote, "The carnal mind is enmity against God; for it is not subject to the law of God, nor indeed can be" (Rom. 8:7). We are born with a rebellious nature, and we are accountable for our deeds performed in rebellion against God's commandments.

Again, guilt is true guilt when it is the by-product of our willful sin. Guilt is false guilt when it is the by-product of another person's willful sin. What should a person do if he discovers that he has been carrying a load of false guilt? He should come before his heavenly Father and say, "I confess that I have been carrying a burden that isn't mine. I give this burden of guilt to You today, Lord Jesus. I turn it over to You completely and ask You to carry it. I receive Your forgiveness, and by my faith, I accept the fact that I am free of this guilt and any aspect of sin associated with it. In Jesus' name, amen!"

꙰ When have you been a participant in a sin against your will? Have you felt guilty?

꙰ When have you deliberately done something that you knew was wrong? Did you feel guilty?

For to be carnally minded is death, but to be spiritually minded is life and peace. Because the carnal mind is enmity against
God; for it is not subject to the law of God, nor indeed can be.

—Romans 8:6–7

✎ What does it mean to be "carnally minded"? To be "spiritually minded"?

✎ Give some real-life examples of being carnally minded. How do those actions display opposition to God?

A Definition of Sin

Some people define *sin* as "missing the mark"—just as an arrow misses a bull's-eye on a target. God's commandments are the target, and we miss God's ideal when we sin. Others define *sin* as "falling short" of God's perfect will. God's desire is that we live in wholeness and follow Him explicitly in all His commandments and directives. We fail to do so in our imperfection, and that is sin. Still others define *sin* as "trespassing." God has areas of behavior that He designates off-limits to us, and we trespass into those territories and are subject to penalty. We have sinned against God and others.

My personal favorite definition of sin comes from Jeremiah 2:13:

> For My people have committed two evils:
> They have forsaken Me, the fountain of living waters,
> And hewn themselves cisterns—broken cisterns that can hold
> no water.

Cisterns are wells that are dug into the earth, usually into solid rock, with the intention of holding water. God is painting a fascinating picture in these words of the prophet. He is saying, "You have rejected Me as a fountain of living water for your life." A fountain is an artesian spring—one that bubbles up from the earth with an unending supply of fresh, pure water. A fountain gives water that is free for the taking.

Jesus encountered a Samaritan woman by the well of Sychar, and in the course of His conversation with her, He said of Himself, "If you knew the gift of God, and who it is who says to you, 'Give Me a drink,' you would have asked Him, and He would have given you living water" (John 4:10). Jesus is painting this same word picture about Himself—He has life to give that is eternal and is freely offered. His forgiveness is a fountain from which we can draw in an unending fashion. His forgiveness is free for the asking.

"But," God says through Jeremiah, "instead of choosing My living water, you have chosen to build cisterns." To build is an act of the will. The cistern builders rejected the artesian spring for a well of their own making. And the Lord noted with sadness but with certainty, "It is a broken well." There is a crack in the cistern, which means that it won't hold the water. "Everything that you do to achieve your own forgiveness is futile," God is saying. "You can dig and dig, you can make cistern after cistern, you can strive and struggle all you want, and it will never bring you forgiveness."

The only forgiveness that we can ever experience is God's forgiveness, granted God's way. Anytime we attempt to meet any of our needs or accomplish anything by means other than God's means, we are setting ourselves up for eventual failure—we are building a broken cistern. If we want to be our own savior rather than accept the Savior whom God has provided, we will fail in our attempt.

∽ Recall, in detail, one time when you willfully chose your way over what you knew to be God's way. What was the result?

For My people have committed two evils: They have forsaken Me, the fountain of living waters, And hewn themselves cisterns--broken cisterns that can hold no water.

—Jeremiah 2:13

∽ Why does God list these sins separately? Put into your own words what these sins are: forsaking God's water, and building your own cistern.

A Willful Choice Against God

Ultimately, people's willful choices against God can form a pattern that leads to eternal death. God doesn't send people to hell—people choose to go there. They choose to trample upon the blood of Jesus; they choose to walk nonchalantly past the cross; they choose to avoid the empty tomb. They choose to ignore the songs of redemption that they have heard a thousand times. They choose to harden their hearts to the prayers of others on their behalf. They choose to turn a deaf ear to sermons that speak of salvation and to the witness of Christ's love from friends and strangers. They choose to ignore and repress the countless promptings of the Holy Spirit tugging at their hearts. They choose to rebel.

People really have to *work* to refuse God's gift of forgiveness—but some do. They refuse to give up their pride and to submit to doing things God's way. They refuse to drink from the fountain of His living water freely made available to them, and they strive instead to build cisterns—cisterns that inevitably will break and fail to satisfy the deep thirst of the soul.

Forgiveness Is a Gift

Throughout the New Testament, forgiveness is pictured as a gift of God. Romans 6:23 tells us, "The wages of sin is death, but the gift of God is eternal life in Christ Jesus our Lord." A gift is free to you; you don't have to do anything to earn it, all you have to do is receive it. That's the way that God offers forgiveness to you. He extends it to you as a gift. You cannot earn your salvation.

Note that the *wages* of sin is death. Death is something that you can earn through repeated disobedience and rejection of God's forgiveness.

41

You can earn the consequences for disobedience, but you can never earn forgiveness. It is God's free gift—His living water. The only thing you have to do to receive forgiveness is to receive forgiveness—and when you do, you truly have made a choice for life.

I invite you to read carefully the words of an Old Testament prophet who knew about the nature of sin, guilt, and the obstinacy of the human will when it is turned against God. Daniel wrote profoundly about sin, yet with the hope and belief that God does and will forgive. Let his words speak to your heart today. Make them your prayer.

> Then I set my face toward the Lord God to make request by prayer and supplications, with fasting, sackcloth, and ashes. And I prayed to the LORD my God, and made confession, and said, "O Lord, great and awesome God, who keeps His covenant and mercy with those who love Him, and with those who keep His commandments, we have sinned and committed iniquity, we have done wickedly and rebelled, even by departing from Your precepts and Your judgments. Neither have we heeded Your servants the prophets, who spoke in Your name to our kings and our princes, to our fathers and all the people of the land. O Lord, righteousness belongs to You, but to us shame of face.

> —Daniel 9:3–7

❧ What does Daniel mean when he says that he "set his face" toward God? How does this compare with the "shame of face" that he also speaks of?

Who are the "servants" and "prophets" that Daniel mentions? In what ways have you failed to listen to them in your life?

What is Daniel's unspoken assumption concerning God's mercy in this prayer? How does this apply to your own need for forgiveness?

Today and Tomorrow

TODAY: GOD'S FORGIVENESS IS A GIFT, AND THERE IS NOTHING THAT I CAN EVER DO TO EARN IT.

TOMORROW: I WILL PRAISE THE LORD FOR HIS FREE GIFT OF MY SALVA- TION.

LESSON 5

What About the Christian Who Sins?

──────── ❧ **In This Lesson** ❧ ────────

LEARNING: DOES IT MEAN THAT I'M NOT SAVED IF I COMMIT SIN?

GROWING: WILL GOD EVER FORGIVE ME FOR WHAT I'VE DONE SINCE BEING SAVED?

A saved person can commit sin—and he or she can also be forgiven. Christians who engage in sin tend to think one of two things. On the one hand are those who say, "Well, I'm saved, so I have eternal security and am going to heaven. God will automatically forgive me of any sins I commit." On the other hand are those who say, "I can't believe that I did that as a Christian. How can God forgive me for this? I don't deserve a second chance or a third chance or a hundredth chance. I'm going to sin again, so how can God ever forgive me?" In this lesson, we will take a look at both approaches.

A License to Sin?

Once people have received the Holy Spirit into their lives, He does not depart from them. God never stops loving them, and He never relinquishes His hold upon people who turn to Him and receive His forgiveness and the indwelling presence of the Holy Spirit. The Lord may appear silent in their lives for a period of time. They may not feel God's presence in a strong way. Nevertheless, the Lord is present in their lives.

Consider the example of the children of Israel throughout the Old Testament. They erred, they made mistakes, they sinned, they repented, and they sinned again. God chastised them, disciplined them, and gave their enemies victory over them on occasion to cause them to turn again to Him. Even so, they were always the children of God, and they never stopped being His people.

The same is true for us as Christians today. We are fully adopted into the same family of God, and God does not disinherit His children. We are not immune to chastisement, discipline, or correction. On the contrary, the Spirit will correct the Father's children whenever necessary to help us stay in line with God's best for us! But we are not subject to abandonment.

Paul wrote to the Romans:

> Who shall separate us from the love of Christ? Shall tribulation, or distress, or persecution, or famine, or nakedness, or peril, or sword? ... For I am persuaded that neither death nor life, nor angels nor principalities nor powers, nor things present nor things to come, nor height nor depth, nor any other created thing, shall be able to separate us from the love of God which is in Christ Jesus our Lord.

> — Romans 8:35, 38–39

Knowing that you can never be separated from the love of Christ, however, is no license to sin. Rather, it is an impetus to live a righteous life. If you are looking for a way to justify your sin, perhaps you should question whether you have ever really received Christ into your life in the first place.

God calls us to holy, righteous, obedient living. Once we truly under-stand forgiveness and the deadly penalty of being in an unpardoned state of sin, we won't want to breach our relationship with God. Our sins will be grievous to us, not enjoyable.

People sometimes misuse this verse: "If we confess our sins, He is faithful and just to forgive us our sins and to cleanse us from all unrigh-teousness" (1 John 1:9). They assume, "Well, I can sin and run to God and ask Him to forgive me, and He will." That's a very casual attitude to have about a matter as serious as sin.

Yes, God will forgive you of your sins when you confess them, but per-haps you should reconsider what confession really means. Confession means that you admit to God that you have erred, you are genuinely sorry for what you have done, and you have no desire to commit the sin in the future. The confession should include a request that God, by the power of His Holy Spirit, will help you never to commit such a sin again. (We'll discuss this in greater depth in the next lesson.)

Forgiveness Produces a Conduct Change

Prior to receiving Jesus Christ as your Savior, you had the natural ten-dency to sin. Sin was automatic for you. Once you have received the life of Christ, however, it is no longer natural for you to sin. Your nature now is to walk in close relationship with God. That's part of what it means to be a "new creation" in Christ Jesus (2 Cor. 5:17).

That doesn't mean that you won't occasionally yield to temptation and commit sin against God or your fellow human beings, but the Holy Spirit will quickly convict you about that sin. Your sin will seem un-natural, odious, and undesirable to you. You will want to receive God's forgiveness and be reconciled to your heavenly Father.

Therefore, if anyone is in Christ, he is a new creation; old things have passed away; behold, all things have become new. Now all things are of God, who has reconciled us to Himself through Jesus Christ, and has given us the ministry of reconciliation.

—2 Corinthians 5:17-18

❧ What "old things" passed away when you became a Christian? Give specific examples from your own life.

❧ In practical terms, what does it mean to be a "new creation"? What does this suggest regarding temptation and sin?

The only thing that tends to stand in the way of forgiveness for the Christian who sins is your questioning whether God will forgive you. Let me assure you, He will if you turn to Him in genuine humility to confess and repent of your sin. How do I know this to be true? The most famous parable of Jesus tells me so.

Our Father Is a Forgiving Father

The parable of the prodigal son should, in my opinion, be called the parable of the forgiving father. The message of this story is of love and forgiveness from start to finish, but we need to recognize that the image of God as a loving Father is not a new one introduced by Jesus. It is a message throughout the Old Testament as well.

Moses knew the gracious love of God when God told him that His "Presence" would go with him and He would give him rest, even after the children of Israel had turned from God in making a golden calf as an idol to worship. (See Ex. 33:14–23.) Nehemiah prayed to God with the full expectation that God would hear his confession on behalf of the children of Israel, forgive their sin, and restore His people to Jerusalem. (See Neh. 1:11.) The psalmist spoke repeatedly of a forgiving God. (See Pss. 51; 130.) Daniel saw forgiveness and mercy as God's very nature. (See Dan. 9:9.)

One of the most vital truths that you can ever learn about God is that He loves you unconditionally, infinitely, and tenderly. His love never changes. It is His nature. God's love and God's desire to forgive are inseparable.

If You, LORD, should mark iniquities, O Lord, who could stand?
But there is forgiveness with You, That You may be feared.

—Psalm 130:3–4

48

↬ The "fear" that the psalmist mentions here is a reverential awe toward God. Why is this a natural response to God's forgiveness?

↬ What does the psalmist mean by "mark iniquities" in these verses? How do we balance this with the fact that God hates sin?

The parable of the forgiving father is found in Luke 15:11–24. Earlier in that same chapter are two other teachings by Jesus about forgiveness. One is the story of a man who has one hundred sheep and loses one of them. He searches for the one lost sheep until he finds it. When he returns home with the lost sheep draped over his shoulders, he calls his friends and neighbors together and says, "Rejoice with me, for I have found my sheep which was lost!"

The second story is about a woman who has ten silver coins. She loses one of them and searches diligently until she finds it. When she has recovered her precious coin, she calls her friends and neighbors together and says, "Rejoice with me, for I have found the piece which I lost!" In both cases, Jesus concludes His parables by saying, "There is joy in heaven over sinners who repent." (See Luke 15:4–10.)

Jesus then tells a third story. As you read this parable in its entirety, I encourage you to circle the word *father* each time you find it.

A certain man had two sons. And the younger of them said to his father, "Father, give me the portion of goods that falls to me." So he divided to them his livelihood. And not many days after, the younger son gathered all together, journeyed to a far country, and there wasted his possessions with prodigal living. But when he had spent all, there arose a severe famine in that land, and he began to be in want. Then he went and joined himself to a citizen of that country, and he sent him into his fields to feed swine. And he would gladly have filled his stomach with the pods that the swine ate, and no one gave him anything. But when he came to himself, he said, "How many of my father's hired servants have bread enough and to spare, and I perish with hunger! I will arise and go to my father, and will say to him, 'Father, I have sinned against heaven and before you, and I am no longer worthy to be called your son. Make me like one of your hired servants.'" And he arose and came to his father. But when he was still a great way off, his father saw him and had compassion, and ran and fell on his neck and kissed him. And the son said to him, "Father, I have sinned against heaven and in your sight, and am no longer worthy to be called your son." But the father said to his servants, "Bring out the best robe and put it on him, and put a ring on his hand and sandals on his feet. And bring the fatted calf here and kill it, and let us eat and be merry; for this my son was dead and is alive again; he was lost and is found." And they began to be merry.

—Luke 15:11–24

Notice that the son is part of the family. He is a good Jewish boy in a good Jewish family. As Christians, our identity can be with this son. He sinned even though he was part of the family. Christians sometimes sin even though we are part of God's family.

❧ What role does the father play in the son's forgiveness? What role does the son play?

❧ Why does the father respond with such joy and generosity when his son returns? How would you have responded if you were the father? If you were the son?

The Motivation for God's Forgiveness

The motivation for forgiveness lies squarely with the father. The younger son says, "I want what I want, and I want it now." He then leaves home with the inheritance that his father gives him. And let me point out to you that the father gave the boy what was going to be legally and rightfully his one day. He didn't deny the boy's request. He didn't override the boy's will. He let the boy go.

God will let you go today if you decide to turn your back on Him and walk away. He will continue to woo you in the deep recesses of your heart and mind, but God never oversteps the boundaries of your will to choose what and whom you want to pursue.

The boy walks away from all the goodness and security that he has known in his father's house—and in so doing, walks out of the will of God for his life. He squanders what he has in loose living, which implies immoral indulgences. This son has squandered his inheritance, money that his father earned. In other words, he has totally wasted all that he once possessed of the father. In our terms today, we would probably conclude that this boy was as backslidden as a person can get. He has no semblance of Christ-likeness left in his behavior. He has lost it all. Anything that he had ever possessed in the way of inheritance from the father, he has wasted away in his sin.

After the boy has squandered his inheritance, he faces a severe famine. Let me assure you, anytime you walk out of the will of God for your life, you *will* walk into a famine, a time of great need. The boy ends up feeding hogs, the most despicable job that any good Jewish boy could have, since hogs are considered unclean by the Jews. Not only that, but hogs in those days were sacrificed by the Romans who occupied the land where Jesus lived and was teaching. Swine were sacrificed to the "god of the netherworld." Their sacrifice was intended to pacify the devil himself. Do you get a picture of just how far this boy has gone from his father and from God?

There is nothing in what this boy has done to earn or motivate God's forgiveness. But that is true for all of us. There is no task or good work that we can do to earn our salvation. Nothing in us is commendable to God. The motivation for forgiving this errant son lies totally within the father, just as the motivation for forgiving sinners lies totally within God.

If you, as a born-again child of God, have sinned and turned from God, there is no good deed that you can do to win yourself back into God's good graces. You can't substitute church attendance, witnessing, committee work, or any form of service for confession of your sins, a request for God's forgiveness, and repentance (a change of your mind and behavior).

When have you acted like the son in this parable? Have you repented of that behavior?

Put the son's prayer of repentance into your own words. Have you prayed something similar in your own life?

The Manifestation of God's Forgiveness

Notice all the ways in this story in which the father responds to what his son has done.

The father sees the son while he is still a long way off. The implication is that the father is looking for him. The father certainly hasn't forgotten his son.

The father has compassion. His heart is filled with tender love and concern for his son. There is no hint that this father has turned against his son or that he feels anything other than great affection toward him.

The father runs to him. No dignified Jewish man ran. It was considered beneath the stature of a wealthy landowner to run. But this father runs to his son. He is eager to embrace his son and welcome him home. He has been waiting in forgiveness for his boy to return home.

The father falls on his son's neck and kisses him. The father embraces his son fully and kisses him repeatedly in Middle Eastern fashion. He is ecstatic at his son's return, and his heart overflows with love. There is no judgment. There are no demands for restitution or accounting. On the contrary, there is no hint of anything but warm acceptance.

The father orders the servants to bring out the best robe for his son, a ring for the son's hand, and sandals for his feet. All of these signal that the boy is a son and not a servant. This boy has just returned from a long journey, and he has come from a debauched lifestyle in which he was slopping hogs. He is a mess. He no doubt smells and looks like the reprobate person he has been.

But the father covers all that with a fine robe. He is not going to have others gawking at his son and belittling him. He immediately restores him to a position of respect. He doesn't say, "Well, you get yourself cleaned up and then we'll talk." He says instead, "Put a robe on my son. The past is the past."

The ring is no doubt a signet ring, which the boy could use to conduct business on his father's behalf. It is as if the father has given his son his personal charge card. The sandals send a signal that the father has no intention of regarding his son in any way other than as a son. In that time, sandals were reserved for family members.

All of these gifts to his son are signs that the father sees his son as a son, a fully restored member of his family. There is nothing that this boy has to do to earn or win his way back into the good graces of his father.

The father tells his servants to kill the fatted calf and prepare a party. The father celebrates the fact that his son has returned home. In an echo of the shepherd who lost a sheep and the woman who lost a valuable coin, this father says, "Let us eat and be merry; for this my son was dead and is alive again; he was lost and is found" (Luke 15:23–24). The father fully expects his son to remain with him and be a faithful son in every regard.

List the things that the father does in this parable to demonstrate his joy. What does this teach about God's love for you?

List the things that the son did to offend his father. What does this teach about God's forgiveness?

55

How Do You Think of Your Heavenly Father?

The father in this parable has been unceasing in his love, patient in his waiting, and willing in his forgiveness. This father is loving in his acceptance and ecstatic at the son's return. This father restores his son completely, holding nothing back—faultlessly, asking for no accounting. Is this your image of your heavenly Father when you sin against Him and against others? Do you see the Father as eager, longing, and completely willing for your return?

Too often we see God as our judge, just waiting to punish us for a wrong that we have committed. Jesus said that God is a loving Father, just waiting to forgive us for the wrongs that we have done.

I also want you to recognize in this story that the father never holds any unforgiveness in his heart. He forgives his son when he asks for his inheritance, when he walks out the door, all the time he is away, upon his return, and in his restoration. The father forgives his son the moment the son begins to move away. The father is forgiving at all times.

So is our heavenly Father. He never stops forgiving us. We are the ones who turn from His commandments. We are the ones who reject His forgiveness. We are the ones who walk away from His presence. The question is not, "Will God forgive me, a Christian, when I sin?" The question is, "Will I receive God's forgiveness for my sin?"

You have put off the old man with his deeds, and have put on the new man who is renewed in knowledge according to the image of Him who created him.

—Colossians 3:9–10

❧ What does it mean to "put off the old man"? Who is the old man? Who is the "new man"?

❧ In practical terms, how do we put off the old man? How do we put on the new man?

❧ Today and Tomorrow ❧

TODAY: GOD IS ALWAYS FORGIVING, ALWAYS WORKING TO BRING US BACK TO HIMSELF.

TOMORROW: I WILL RUN BACK TO MY FATHER WHEN I SIN, KNOWING THAT HE WILL RECEIVE ME.

LESSON 6

What Role Does Confession Play?

---------------- ❧ **In This Lesson** ☙ ----------------

LEARNING: WHAT IS THE DIFFERENCE BETWEEN REPENTANCE AND CONFESSION?

GROWING: WILL GOD KEEP FORGIVING ME, AGAIN AND AGAIN?

---------------- ∞ ----------------

You may be saying at this point in your study of sin and forgiveness, "Well, what is our part? Isn't there anything that we have to do?"

Yes, we must do something as part of the process of receiving forgiveness. The pattern for receiving forgiveness is also evident in the story of the forgiving father, which we discussed in the last lesson. Let me remind you of these verses:

> But when he [the son] came to himself, he said, "How many of my father's hired servants have bread enough and to spare, and I perish with hunger! I will arise and go to my father, and will say to him, 'Father, I have sinned against heaven and before you, and I am no longer worthy to be called your son. Make me like one of your hired servants.' " And he arose and came to his father.... And the son said to him, "Father, I have sinned against heaven and in your sight, and am no longer worthy to be called your son."
>
> —Luke 15:17–21

This boy "came to himself." We might say, "He came to his senses." He began to think the right way, and he began to have a clear picture of himself, his sin, and his father. He started to think the truth about his situation—that even his father's servants were better off than he was. Furthermore, his attitude was summed up in this statement: "Father, I have sinned against heaven and in your sight."

Recognizing the truth—and agreeing with it—is called *confession*. Confession is vital to receiving forgiveness. To *confess* means to "agree." It involves our thinking and admitting to God, "You're right, I've sinned. I'm a sinner. I have not only wronged other people and myself, but I have wronged heaven."

As long as you refuse to admit that you have done wrong, you can't be forgiven. God is willing to forgive you, but if you refuse to admit that you have done wrong, you won't turn to Him and receive His forgiveness.

Why does the son say that he will "arise"? What "arising" is required if we are to repent of sin?

Why does the son say that he has sinned against heaven and in his father's sight? What does this teach about the nature of all sin?

I have cited this verse before, but it's worth repeating: "If we confess our sins, He is faithful and just to forgive us our sins and to cleanse us from all unrighteousness" (1 John 1:9). Your forgiveness begins when you confess your sins, admitting to God that you have done wrong and that you are out of fellowship with Him.

God already knows that you have done wrong. He knows what you did the moment you did it. He knows your thoughts, your motivations, your intent, your will. The sins that you confess aren't news to God. Furthermore, if you are a Christian and you sin, God has already forgiven you. Romans 8:1 is an important verse for every Christian to memorize: "There is therefore now no condemnation to those who are in Christ Jesus, who do not walk according to the flesh, but according to the Spirit." In other words, your confession doesn't cause God to forgive you. In confessing, you aren't talking God into forgiveness. He has already forgiven you.

Anytime Paul referred to forgiveness in his letters, he put forgiveness in the past tense. He reminded the Ephesians that Christ "forgave" them and they were "sealed" by the Holy Spirit (see Eph. 4:30–32). He reminded the Colossians that they were the elect of God and "raised" with Christ (see Col. 3). God has already forgiven you. No amount of confessing can talk God into something that is already His desire.

What is the purpose of confession if God already knows that you have sinned, and is willing to forgive you? The purpose is for you to come to grips with what you have done and the position that you are in. Confession is a reality check, and it's the key to your receiving forgiveness into your own life and experiencing the freedom that forgiveness brings.

If you do not admit to yourself and to God what you have done, you will not be able to experience what God desires to give you: release from guilt and shame, and new freedom to walk boldly in your relationship with Him. You confess so that you can experience the forgiveness that has been available to you all along, so you can enter fully into relationship with God, and so you can correct your behavior.

Let's say that I left my watch on the pulpit, where I laid it while I was preaching. You come along and take it and wear it as your own. You know that you've stolen the watch and you feel a little uneasy about that, but you aren't too concerned because you don't think your sin will ever be revealed.

Word comes to me, your pastor, that you have my watch, and my response is one of immediate forgiveness. I refuse to hold this act against you. I choose to cancel any debt associated with your deed. (Remember, that is what forgiveness is—it's a release, a cancellation of any debt.)

Because I have forgiven you and freed you of any debt, I assume the loss of my watch. The person who forgives always assumes the loss. That's part of canceling the debt. Because I have canceled any debt regarding your wrongdoing, I can meet you in the hallway of the church and be friendly and warm with you. As far as I am concerned, your action is without any consequence to me.

Then someone comes to you and says, "The pastor knows that you stole his watch." You are likely to be very uncomfortable—even more so than you were before. You knew that you were the thief, but you didn't know that anybody else knew—and you certainly didn't know that I, your pastor, knew about it. Suddenly, you do whatever you can to ignore me and avoid me. You feel strange in my presence.

Your friend comes to you again and says, "The pastor has forgiven you for stealing his watch." That has little impact on you. You think, "Well, maybe he has, but I'm not certain." Your sin continues to fester until you can't stand it any longer. Finally, you come to me and say, "Pastor, here's your watch. I took it from the pulpit, and I'm sorry. I know I've done wrong."

We have a time of reconciliation. I have already forgiven you, but now you are able to receive my forgiveness. Our relationship is restored, and in all likelihood, we are closer than ever.

> Confess your trespasses to one another, and pray for one another, that you may be healed. The effective, fervent prayer of a righteous man avails much.

> —James 5:16

When have you confessed a sin to another person? How did it affect your relationship?

When has someone confessed a sin to you? Did you forgive that person? How did it affect the relationship?

The confession of the prodigal son didn't cause the father to forgive him. The father had already done so! But it did put the son into a position where he might receive his father's forgiveness and be comfortable and free in his relationship with his father.

Asking for God's Forgiveness

Asking for God's forgiveness is likely to be part of your confession. The prodigal son does not ask directly for his father to forgive him, but the request is implied in his saying, "Make me like one of your hired servants." The son doesn't expect that his father will restore him completely, but he does believe that his father will at the very least take him back as a hired servant. In so doing, his father will have forgiven him to a degree. The son, of course, is in for a wonderful surprise: the father forgives him fully. The heavenly Father knows that in your confession of your sin you are implicitly asking for Him to forgive you. And He will. Even so, you benefit by asking.

Jesus asked a blind man who came to Him, "What do you want Me to do for you?" (See Mark 10:46–52.) Jesus certainly could see that Bartimaeus was blind. Bartimaeus knew that Jesus knew. Yet Jesus asked him the question anyway. The question was not for Jesus' information. It was for Bartimaeus' sake, that he would realize fully what he was requesting of God. With sight would come all sorts of responsibilities for Bartimaeus. He would have to work for his living rather than beg. He would have to be responsible for his care rather than rely on the constant help of others. Jesus no doubt wanted to make certain that Bartimaeus knew fully what he was asking.

The same thing holds true for us. When we state openly and directly what we have done as a sin, and we ask openly and directly for forgiveness of that sin, we are much more likely to face our sin and determine within ourselves that we will not sin again. In like manner, when we first come to the Lord for forgiveness, and we state openly that we are sinners, we are much more likely to determine that we will live our lives in a new way and walk in a new direction.

If you say, "O Lord, I lied to Mary today about what Jane said, and I know I did wrong in Your sight, and I ask You to forgive me," you are brought face-to-face in a powerful way with your sin, its consequences, and your need for forgiveness. You walk away from such a prayer with appreciation for God's forgiveness, and you walk away with conviction from God's Holy Spirit about how you are to make things right with Mary!

Asking for God's forgiveness does not force God to forgive you—He already has done so out of His motivation of unconditional love—but it does make you more acutely aware of what you are asking, who you are addressing when you make your request, and what might be the actions that God wants you to take.

> If you confess with your mouth the Lord Jesus and believe in your heart that God has raised Him from the dead, you will be saved. For with the heart one believes unto righteousness, and with the mouth confession is made unto salvation.
>
> —Romans 10:9–10

What role is played by the heart in these verses? What role is played by the mouth? Why are both important?

What conditions must we fill to receive righteousness? To receive salvation?

The Importance of Asking with Faith

As you make your confession and ask God to forgive you, do so with faith, fully trusting God to hear your confession and to forgive you. *Believing* for forgiveness is a part of *receiving* forgiveness. If you don't believe that God is going to forgive you, you won't receive forgiveness, and you won't experience freedom from guilt's bondage. You must believe that God is going to be true to His Word and forgive you when you confess your sins and ask Him for forgiveness.

If you have never confessed your sins to God before, you must believe that when you do, God is going to hear your confession and immediately transfer you from the kingdom of darkness to the kingdom of God. (See Acts 26:18.) You must believe that you are no longer a victim of Satan, but a child of God. You must believe that God has freed you from all bondage of sin and its guilt, and that you are now free to walk in full fellowship with Him, living in righteousness and enjoying all the benefits of reconciliation with Him.

For you were once darkness, but now you are light in the Lord. Walk as children of light (for the fruit of the Spirit is in all goodness, righteousness, and truth).

—Ephesians 5:8-9

🖎 What does it mean to "walk as children of light"? Give practical examples.

🖎 What does truth have to do with confession of sin? What truth can we claim when we do confess sin?

If you are a Christian, when you confess your sin and ask God to forgive you, you must believe that God has forgiven you and restored you to full fellowship with Him. It is by faith that you can say to the Lord as you confess and ask for forgiveness, "I receive what Jesus Christ did for me on the cross. I receive Your forgiveness into my life. I receive the gift of Your Holy Spirit. I receive Your full embrace of love and Your call to follow You in the paths of righteousness."

Ask, and it will be given to you; seek, and you will find; knock, and it will be opened to you. For everyone who asks receives, and he who seeks finds, and to him who knocks it will be opened.

—Matthew 7:7–8

🔖 Why does the Lord speak of asking, seeking, and knocking regarding confession? What do these actions imply about confession of sin?

🔖 Who will receive forgiveness, according to these verses? What guarantee do you have?

Does Confession Keep Us Forgiven?

Some people think that confession keeps them in a state of forgiveness—if they continually confess what they have done, they'll be able to ward off any consequences of bad behavior. They use it as a defense. That isn't the purpose of confession, and that isn't the way that confession works. You may still face consequences for your sinful behavior while you were in rebellion against God.

The story of the prodigal son shifts focus after the son returns home to become the story of the brother who stayed at home. As part of that story, we find the father telling the elder son, "Son, you are always with me, and all that I have is yours" (Luke 15:31). The father is stating, "All the inheritance remaining is yours and always has been." The prodigal son doesn't get a second inheritance to replace the one that he has squandered. He has the full rights and privileges of living as a son in his father's house, but he also must live with the fact that he has squandered his original inheritance.

Repeated confession doesn't ward off consequences. If we think that it does, we haven't truly repented as part of our confession.

> But let him ask in faith, with no doubting, for he who doubts is like a wave of the sea driven and tossed by the wind.
>
> —James 1:6

❧ Describe the characteristics of waves during a strong wind storm. How does that picture apply to someone who repeatedly asks forgiveness for the same sins?

❧ James is speaking of asking for wisdom in this verse. What part does wisdom play in confession and repentance?

The Role of Repentance

To *repent* means to "change your mind and behavior." Repentance is an act of the will. It involves follow-through behavior. Confession is an admission; it is saying, "I have sinned." Repentance takes that confession and puts it into action. It is declaring, "I am changing my mind and my behavior so that I will not sin again." Repentance involves the actual doing of what we say we are going to do.

The prodigal son said, "I will arise and go to my father," and two verses later we read, "He arose and came to his father" (18, 20). The prodigal son changed his mind, he made a decision about a change in his behavior which included a change in his circumstances and location, and then he acted on that decision. That's repentance. Repentance doesn't bring you into a forgiven, guilt-free relationship with the Father. Confession and asking God to forgive you does that, and repentance keeps you there.

Too many people believe that they must repent of their sins before God will forgive them. No! We repent of our sins *because* the Father forgives us, and *as* the Father forgives us He enables us by the presence of His Holy Spirit. Our change of behavior doesn't happen before we come to God and receive His forgiveness. If that was the case, repentance would be filled with all sorts of works—good deeds to do, points to earn, obstacles to overcome. Our declaration that we intend to change our behavior and not sin again may be part of our confession, but the real change in our behavior comes *after* we have received God's forgiveness.

Thank God that it does, because when we are in full reconciliation with God, we are more likely to avail ourselves of the full power of the Holy Spirit working in us to help us stay true to our commitment and to live a sin-free life. Repentance allows us to walk in abundant grace and in God's gift of righteousness, which He promises to us as part of our forgiveness (Rom. 5:17). Repentance is our decision to follow God, followed by our change of behavior that keeps us on God's path.

Honest confession admits sin and asks for God's forgiveness, and repentance defines a necessary change in behavior to live a righteous life; makes a declaration that one is going to pursue that change; and then follows through with actual change. To confess without repentance is to say, "I'm sorry," without any effort to sin no more. Genuine repentance—the desire and action *not* to sin again—validates confession. The two are inseparable for any person who desires to walk in close fellowship with God.

When have you confessed a sin to the Lord without really intending to abandon that sin in the future? What was the result?

When have you determined in your heart to stop committing some sinful act in the future? What was the result?

How Often Should You Confess?

Confession should be continual. Anytime that you recognize sin in your life, you must come to God and confess it. This isn't so that your salvation can be kept current and up-to-date, but so that you can live and walk in continual freedom and intimacy with the Father.

✎ How Often Should You Confess the Same Sin? ✎

That depends on how often you commit it. Each time you sin, you should confess it to God and ask His forgiveness. If you are involved in repeated confessions for the same types of behavior, you should ask yourself, "Have I really repented of this? Am I making the effort of my will to change my mind and change my behavior? Am I relying on the Holy Spirit to help me *not* to sin?"

To sin repeatedly is an act of your will. So is repentance. Your will is within your power. You *can* change your mind, your behavior, your actions, and your words, and if you ask the Holy Spirit to help you, He will!

On the other hand, you need to confess a specific act of sin only once, and God hears your confession and forgives you. It doesn't matter how awful or how big your sin has been, God is able to forgive it in one moment!

Confession and Intimacy with God

Ultimately, full confession has to do with restoring and maintaining intimacy with God. The Lord wants to walk in close fellowship with you today. He longs to have a walking-and-talking-together relationship with you.

Confess to the Lord that you have done things, said things, thought things, and believed things that make you uncomfortable in His presence. Ask Him to forgive you for your sins and to remove your feelings of guilt and discomfort in His presence. Believe with your faith that He not only hears your request but also grants it fully. And then walk with the Lord! Talk to Him. Share your life with Him, and invite Him to share His life with you.

Confession opens the way to receiving forgiveness and enjoying a close relationship with your loving heavenly Father. Confession is vital to your awareness of His presence, and it should be continual.

> The Lord is not slack concerning His promise, as some count slackness, but is longsuffering toward us, not willing that any should perish but that all should come to repentance.
>
> —2 Peter 3:9

When has the Lord been longsuffering to you? Give specific examples.

What "promise" is Peter referring to here? Have you claimed that promise in your own life?

❧ Today and Tomorrow ❧

TODAY: GOD IS ALWAYS FORGIVING, EVEN WHEN I AM STILL IN SIN.

TOMORROW: I WILL BE MORE FAITHFUL IN REPENTING OF SIN, NOT JUST IN CONFESSING IT.

❧ Notes and Prayer Requests: ❧

LESSON 7

Forgiving Undeserved Injuries

❧ In This Lesson ❧

LEARNING: WHY SHOULD I FORGIVE A PERSON WHO HURTS ME UNJUSTLY?

GROWING: HOW CAN I LET GO OF PAST HURTS?

Unforgiveness is an issue that nearly all of us have to deal with at some point. Unforgiveness that is allowed to remain in our spirits is both painful and destructive. I consider it to be the major root of many physical, emotional, and spiritual problems today.

The apostle Paul wrote to the Ephesians: "Let all bitterness, wrath, anger, clamor, and evil speaking be put away from you, with all malice. And be kind to one another, tenderhearted, forgiving one another, even as God in Christ forgave you" (Eph. 4:31–32). Paul was describing the manifestations of a "spirit of unforgiveness" when he spoke of bitterness, wrath, anger, clamor, and evil speaking. A spirit of unforgiveness goes beyond a temporary state of unforgiveness, which is the period between the time that a person is hurt and the time that he forgives the one who has hurt him. A spirit of unforgiveness develops when he chooses to remain in a state of unforgiveness toward a person who has wronged him.

A spirit of unforgiveness is summed up in this remark: "I don't think I could ever forgive that." We feel that we have been dealt with in such an unjust, harmful way that we can't let go of the pain. We need to face the fact that we are all going to be hurt. We have been hurt, are hurting now, or are going to be hurt by somebody in some area. The only way that we can insulate ourselves against being hurt is to remove ourselves completely from the possibility of love. To risk love is to risk hurt.

Unforgiveness is a choice that we make with the will—and it's a bad choice.

Unforgiveness Is Hatred

Unforgiveness is actually a form of hatred. You may say, "I don't hate anybody." By such a statement, you probably mean that you wouldn't murder anybody or do anything intentionally to harm another person. But ask yourself these questions: Do I avoid encountering a certain person? Do I find it difficult to speak well of a certain person? Does the very thought of a particular person make me cringe or clench my fist? If your answer is yes, you are harboring hatred in the form of unforgiveness.

Hatred exists in degrees. An unforgiving spirit is marked by hatred, and you know that you have such a spirit if:

> you can't shake the painful memory of a hurt done to you.

> you can't honestly wish the offending person well.

> you want the other person to feel pain and suffering to the degree that you have felt them.

If this describes you, face up to the fact that you have a degree of hatred in you for that person, and you have a spirit of unforgiveness.

⮞ Has a particular person or past injury come to your mind in this lesson? Is the Lord showing you an area of unforgiveness?

Eventual Consequences

Unforgiveness will take one of two forms in your life. Either you will stuff it inside you and keep it bottled up, where it will turn to bitterness and resentment; or you will actively seek to retaliate against the person, taking vengeance in your own hands to repay the wrong done to you. Either way, you will be the victim of your unforgiveness far more than the person who has wronged you.

There is a way out of this condition, however! You can choose to forgive the person. Nobody can make you have an unforgiving spirit. It is an act of your will, a choice that you make. You can also choose by your will to forgive.

Commanded to Forgive

You should choose to forgive just for your own health and well-being, but you are also commanded by the Lord to make that choice. God's commandments are always for our good, and this one is no exception.

Jesus plainly taught, "If you forgive men their trespasses, your heavenly Father will also forgive you. But if you do not forgive men their trespasses, neither will your Father forgive your trespasses" (Matt. 6:14–15). If you want to experience God's forgiveness, you must forgive others.

> Love your enemies, do good to those who hate you, bless those who curse you, and pray for those who spitefully use you. To him who strikes you on the one cheek, offer the other also. And from him who takes away your cloak, do not withhold your tunic either. Give to everyone who asks of you. And from him who takes away your goods do not ask them back.
>
> —Luke 6:27–30

What sorts of crimes and injuries are covered by these verses? Which of them have been done to you?

Which of those injuries have you done to others?

Reasons for an Unforgiving Spirit

People have an unforgiving spirit for three main reasons.

1. Pride. We simply don't want to forgive because we believe that in some way, forgiving the other person will diminish us. We're afraid that people will think we're weak. In other cases, we may not want to admit that we've been hurt, or to confess that we are finding it difficult to forgive. We fear that people will look down on us for feeling hurt or for having an area of weakness in our spiritual lives. And in still other cases, we may enjoy the attention and consolation that we receive from others who know that we have been wronged. To forgive would be to step out of the limelight of their concern. In all of these cases, our unforgiveness stems from pride.

2. Control. This is closely linked to pride. We want to make sure that the person who has wronged us is punished in the way we choose. The only way that we can ensure that is to hold on to the person, even if it's only holding on to the person in our hearts. We refuse to let go and leave the person in God's hands.

3. Ignorance. Some people don't know how to respond to old hurts and painful situations. They have never been taught how to forgive and so they haven't forgiven. Others have a faulty understanding of what it means to forgive. Also, nonbelievers find it difficult to forgive others fully because they have not experienced forgiveness from God in their own lives. God's forgiveness to us is the model for our forgiveness of others. And in part, it is because of the power of the Holy Spirit in our lives that we are enabled to forgive and release another person fully.

If you are struggling today with unforgiveness, ask yourself why you refuse to free the other person. What compels you to hang on to that hurt and memory?

What comes out of a man, that defiles a man. For from within, out of the heart of men, proceed evil thoughts, adulteries, fornications, murders, thefts, covetousness, wickedness, deceit, lewdness, an evil eye, blasphemy, pride, foolishness. All these evil things come from within and defile a man.

—Mark 7:20–23

In what way do these sins come "from within"? What is "within" us that produces these sins?

How does this principle apply to bitterness versus forgiveness? What is "within" us that produces bitterness? What produces forgiveness?

Our Hurt Can Cause Us to Hurt Others

Our pride and desire for control are at the heart of our trying to have the upper hand over the person who has wronged us, to seek an advantage over the one who has caused us hurt. Our hurt can also cause us to take out our bitterness and resentment on others, even those who may not have hurt us directly.

Jesus taught a parable to illustrate this point:

> Therefore the kingdom of heaven is like a certain king who wanted to settle accounts with his servants. And when he had begun to settle accounts, one was brought to him who owed him ten thousand talents. But as he was not able to pay, his master commanded that he be sold, with his wife and children and all that he had, and that payment be made. The servant therefore fell down before him, saying, "Master, have patience with me, and I will pay you all." Then the master of that servant was moved with compassion, released him, and forgave him the debt. But that servant went out and found one of his fellow servants who owed him a hundred denarii; and he laid hands on him and took him by the throat, saying, "Pay me what you owe!" So his fellow servant fell down at his feet and begged him, saying, "Have patience with me, and I will pay you all." And he would not, but went and threw him into prison till he should pay the debt. So when his fellow servants saw what had been done, they were very grieved, and came and told their master all that had been done. Then the master, after he had called him, said to him, "You wicked servant! I forgave you all that debt because you begged me. Should you not also have had compassion on your fellow servant, just as I had pity on you?" And his master was angry, and delivered him to the torturers until he should pay all that was due to him. So My

heavenly Father also will do to you if each of you, from his heart, does not forgive his brother his trespasses.

—Matthew 18:23–35

🕭 Which servant in this parable do you sympathize with more: the one forgiven by the king, or the who owed a hundred denarii?

🕭 Which servant do you *resemble* more?

No Right to Harbor Unforgiveness

No one has a right to harbor unforgiveness. The Cross strips us of that right. Jesus Christ was pure, sinless, without any shadow of deceit, yet He died on the cross to forgive you. You have no right to deny that forgiveness to another person who is in the same position that you have been in: a sinner in need of forgiveness and salvation.

Forgiveness of others is essential. There may be excuses for us to harbor unforgiveness, but no excuse is a justifiable reason before our heavenly Father. He commands us to forgive.

∾ Why did the king forgive the servant who owed him ten thousand talents? Why did he throw him into prison later?

∾ What is Jesus saying will happen to an unforgiving Christian?

The Consequences of an Unforgiving Spirit

I'll list four consequences of an unforgiving spirit:

1. You will experience emotional bondage. Your memories may torment you, causing you to relive again and again the pain that you have experienced. You very likely will find that you have little capacity to love others or to receive love. Intimacy may be difficult for you.

2. You will experience damaged relationships. You are likely to have relationships marked by anger and fighting—sometimes with what seem to be volcanic eruptions.

3. You will suffer damage in your relationship with the Lord. The Holy Spirit will continually bring your unforgiveness to your mind until you deal with it. You will feel deep restlessness and uneasiness in your spirit until you do. Furthermore, the Holy Spirit cannot anoint unforgiveness. Your ability to minister to others will be stunted.

4. You will suffer damage to your physical being. Unforgiveness puts an overload on the nervous system, and eventually a fuse will blow in some area of your body. The physical body was not designed by God to endure the long-standing stress caused by a spirit of unforgiveness.

But there is good news! You don't need to have a spirit of unforgiveness.

How to Deal with Unforgiveness

The first step in dealing with unforgiveness is identifying the person who has hurt you. It may be someone that you encounter frequently or someone who lives miles away. It may be someone close to you or someone who has died.

I suggest that you weigh carefully whether to confront a person about the hurt caused to you. Your parents, for example, have probably done the best they knew how in raising you, and confronting them with old hurts is only going to wound them, not remedy your current feelings. Your dealings with your hurt should never bring hurt to someone else.

Conduct a confrontation with the person "by proxy." Take two chairs—one for you, and an empty one to represent the other person. Then sit down and talk to that empty chair as if the person is sitting in it. Be true to your feelings. Let out all your hurt. You may cry, shout, even kick the chair! Don't hold anything back. In the course of speaking to the "person," identify the hurt that you feel. Be specific in how you feel and how much you hurt. And identify the debt—cite specific examples, such as places, times, events, and conversations in which the person hurt you.

You may need several sessions to let out all your pain. Your conversation may last for several hours. Spend whatever time it takes to air your full grievance against the person. Then draw a line between all that you have said of your pain and the hurt that has occurred in the past. Declare, "By the grace of God, I release you today. I refuse to hold these things in my heart and memory any longer. I choose to be free of the pain that you have caused me."

Ask the Lord to help you. Confess to Him that you have harbored a spirit of unforgiveness. Ask Him to forgive you for your unforgiveness. Ask Him to release you of the pain as you take these steps. And believe, by faith, that He will do so. Choose to take a new direction in your life, one that is free of pain and bondage associated with old hurts and past suffering.

If you continue to think of things that the hurtful party has said or done, do the exercise again. If other people come to mind, give them a turn in the empty chair. If you have a spirit of unforgiveness, you may very well need to forgive several people. Deal with each person who has hurt you.

The results of taking this act of your will are these:

Your memory begins to be healed. You will think less and less often of the offending person, and each time with less hurt.

You begin to see the person that you have forgiven in a new light. You are likely to see the person that you have forgiven as a sinner in need of God's forgiveness, and you likely will have more compassion for him or her.

You begin to experience freedom in your emotions and in your ability to relate to other people. You are no longer in bondage to that person and you are likely to feel free to relate to other people more readily. If you have been afraid to risk loving another person, you likely will have the courage and strength to take that risk.

You may also experience reconciliation with the person that you have forgiven. That isn't always the case, but sometimes it is possible for there to be a coming together again in friendship or love.

Again, if you choose to remain in unforgiveness, the effects are like a slow poison that works in the soul and spirit. An unforgiving spirit is always corruptive, destructive, and degenerative. Choose to be free of the bondage associated with unforgiveness. Choose to forgive!

> Pursue peace with all people, and holiness, without which no one will see the Lord: looking carefully lest anyone fall short of the grace of God; lest any root of bitterness springing up cause trouble, and by this many become defiled.
>
> —Hebrews 12:14–15

What is a "root of bitterness"? How does it "spring up"? How is it rooted out?

How does a "root of bitterness" cause people to become defiled? Give practical examples.

Beloved, do not avenge yourselves, but rather give place to wrath; for it is written, "VENGEANCE IS MINE, I WILL REPAY," says the Lord. Therefore "IF YOUR ENEMY IS HUNGRY, FEED HIM; IF HE IS THIRSTY, GIVE HIM A DRINK; FOR IN SO DOING YOU WILL HEAP COALS OF FIRE ON HIS HEAD."

—Romans 12:19–20

What does it mean to "give place to wrath"? How is this the opposite of vengeance?

What does it mean to "heap coals of fire" on your enemy's head? How is this different from seeking revenge?

Today and Tomorrow

TODAY: IT IS VITALLY IMPORTANT THAT I ROOT OUT BITTERNESS AND FORGIVE OTHERS.

TOMORROW: I WILL ASK THE LORD TO SHOW ME WHERE A ROOT OF BITTERNESS MIGHT BE GROWING.

LESSON 8

Developing a Forgiving Spirit

─────── ❧ **In This Lesson** ❧ ───────

LEARNING: WHY DO I KEEP COMING AROUND TO STRUGGLING WITH RE-
SENTMENT AGAIN?

GROWING: HOW CAN I BREAK THE CYCLE OF UNFORGIVENESS AND FORGIVE-
NESS?

❧

Forgiveness is an act of the will, as I have stated several times in this study. It's difficult to operate in a rational way, out of the will, when we are being swallowed up by painful, sometimes agonizing emotions. When we are wronged, our natural instinct is to blast our way out of the hurt (with an outburst of anger and hatred) or to bury the hurt (resulting in eventual bitterness and resentment).

The good news is that we can trust the Holy Spirit to help us not act on our natural instincts. In those brief moments before we cry, explode, or steel ourselves against the pain, we can breathe a quick prayer, "Holy Spirit, help me to respond as Jesus would respond. Help me to forgive."

The Cycle of Unforgiveness and Forgiveness

There seems to be a twelve-part cycle of unforgiveness and forgiveness that many people experience. Let me describe each of its steps to you:

87

1. We feel wronged. We feel hurt by another person, who may have committed a trespass intentionally or unintentionally. The person does not even have to have sinned against us for us to feel hurt. The hurt is our response to a situation, event, or conversation. We may feel wronged whether we should feel that way or not.

2. We have difficulty dealing with our hurt. The hurt lingers. The situation matters to us; the pain is great; the suffering is ongoing. We struggle with our feelings.

3. We try to take a detour away from the hurt. Our first response when we are hurt is to flee. We want the pain to go away, so we try to move away from it. We try various substitutes to forgiveness in order to feel better.

4. We deny the pain. We try to convince ourselves that the hurt doesn't matter or that we aren't really hurting.

5. We dig a hole for the pain. When we discover that we cannot outmaneuver our pain—either by taking a detour away from it or denying it—we attempt to bury the pain. We refuse to talk about it and try to forget it. We repress the pain.

6. We feel defeated. We conclude that the person who offended us has scored a victory over us. We have a sense of bitterness and resentment about that.

When have you experienced these steps?

—Wronged

—Struggle

—Detour

—Denial

—Repression/Burial

—Defeat

At this point we probably have developed a spirit of unforgiveness. The cycle continues:

7. We experience defilement. The pain that we have buried within us taints or stains (defiles) our relationships with others. We have shorter tempers, less compassion. We are less willing to risk giving and receiving love.

8. We become discouraged about life. Without freedom in our ability to relate to others, and without freedom and a sense of victory in ourselves, we become discouraged and may even become clinically depressed. We experience no peace, on the inside or the outside.

9. We become desperate. The pain continues to simmer inside us until we reach the point where we are desperate for relief. We want a way out of our misery.

✎ When have you experienced these steps?

—Defilement

—Discouragement

—Desperation

When we are desperate, we are in a very vulnerable state. We are likely to act irrationally and without clear discernment. This is a dangerous state in which to live.

10. We enter into destructive behavior, or we attempt to discover the root cause of what is causing our pain. People who are desperate often turn to drugs, alcohol, pain killers, or sleeping pills for would-be relief from pain—a course of action that leads only to the further pain of addiction. Those who are desperate sometimes seek to escape the life they have known; they may divorce, run away, join communes filled with other desperate people, or engage in occult practices. They may commit suicide. Each avenue is a manifestation of self-destructive behavior.

Outright destructive behavior may also occur. Someone may take revenge on the person that he regards as the source of his pain, causing the person physical harm or doing all within his power to destroy the person's reputation.

Not all who are desperate, however, choose avenues of destruction. In desperation, some turn to therapy and counseling to get to the root cause of their pain. They turn to God, church, prayer groups, and Bible studies, or to the Word of God for solace, advice, and relief of their pain.

☙ When have you been at this crisis point in your pain? What course of action did you take? What were the results?

People who choose a destructive course of action nearly always recognize that they have chosen a dead-end avenue, and they turn to counseling, therapy, or other positive means of discovery. Not all therapists or counselors are godly. Eventually, the counsel of God's Word and the power of the Holy Spirit are going to free a person from this vicious cycle, so we assume that a person who is honestly seeking answers will be led by the Holy Spirit to godly counselors and godly wisdom. That certainly should be our prayer for ourselves or for others who find themselves in a desperate state and who begin to make a positive attempt to discover the root cause of their desperation.

11. We begin to deal with the cause of our pain for what it is—a state of unforgiveness. Ultimately, the cause of our pain in this cycle is our inability or failure to forgive. We may struggle in our attempts to rationalize, justify, or explain the many reasons why we haven't forgiven another person. But in the end, each of us comes face-to-face with this fact: I must forgive to be free.

12. We experience deliverance from our pain as we forgive. We forgive and experience God's release from bondage, guilt, and the spirit of unforgiveness.

☜ When have you experienced these steps?

—Dealing with the pain (and facing issues of unforgiveness)

—Deliverance from the pain (as you forgave)

The Sinner's Cycle

I have described this cycle in terms of forgiving another person, but the same cycle exists for sinners and for those who struggle to forgive themselves. Let me briefly give you those stages:

1. Wronged. We have an awareness that we are living in a state of sin with a nature of sin and are thus separated from God.

2. Struggle. We struggle with the fact that we are sinners.

3. Detour. We try to ignore the inner struggle.

4. Denial. We try to convince ourselves that we are not really sinners.

5. Repression. We try to avoid the issue altogether and turn to other pursuits and activities.

6. Defeat. We live with a sense that we never quite measure up. We may have a wariness of others or an abiding sense of failure.

7. Defilement. We are unable to enter fully into godly relationships. We avoid people that we perceive as "too spiritual" or ones who speak often of God.

8. Discouragement. We have no peace inside. We feel inner tumult and a sense of futility about life.

9. Desperation. We reach the point where we *must* do something about our feelings.

10. Destruction or discovery. We turn and run from God as fast as we can, and as far as we can. Or we turn toward God and begin to explore who He is, what He has said, and why He loves us.

11. Dealing with the pain. We face the fact that we are sinners in need of God's salvation. We confess this to ourselves and to God, ask God for His forgiveness, and decide that we are going to live in accordance with God's plan for our lives.

12. Deliverance. We receive God's forgiveness and are delivered from sin and its guilt and pain. We begin a new life in fellowship with our heavenly Father and with the help of the Holy Spirit.

All sinners who come to the Father for forgiveness go through this cycle, although not all may experience all stages as profoundly, and not all may linger as long in any one stage as others do.

☙ Have you accepted God's free gift of forgiveness through Christ? If not, which step (above) are you on?

☙ If you have received Christ as your Savior, recount the process by which you found deliverance from sin.

The Christian's Cycle of Self-Recrimination and Self-Forgiveness

1. **Wronged.** We have an awareness that we have sinned against God.

2. **Struggle.** We struggle with the fact that we have failed God after He has so generously forgiven us of our sinful nature and called us His children.

3. **Detour.** We try to ignore the inner struggle that we feel and dismiss it.

4. **Denial.** We try to convince ourselves that we have not sinned significantly, or that God will forgive us of our sin automatically without any confession on our part.

5. **Repression.** We continue in the Christian life as if nothing has happened.

6. **Defeat.** We have a deep inner feeling that the devil has defeated us or that we have defeated ourselves. We fear that we may never have a fully restored relationship with God.

7. **Defilement.** We are unable to minister to others freely.

8. **Discouragement.** We become void of hope that things might get better.

9. **Desperation.** We feel that we *must* do something.

10. **Destruction or discovery.** We run from God and God's people as fast as we can, or we turn toward God and begin to explore the possibility of His forgiveness.

11. Dealing with the pain. We face the fact that we have sinned before God, believing that He will forgive us as we confess our sin to Him, ask for His forgiveness, and make a decision to move forward in our lives and, with help from the Holy Spirit, not sin again.

12. Deliverance. We receive God's forgiveness, are delivered from our sin and the pain of our guilt and shame, and live in restored fellowship with the Father, according to His commandments.

🐾 When have you found it difficult to forgive yourself for something that you have done? Did you experience this cycle?

Shortening the Cycle

Many people take years to move through these stages. They may experience many sleepless nights and stress-related illnesses. Some spend a great deal of money in various pursuits to assuage their guilt or shame, and others spend thousands of dollars in therapy. Is there a way to shorten this cycle? Yes!

You can move directly from stage one to stage eleven—from feeling the pain of being wronged to dealing with the pain. Don't take any detours. Don't engage in denial. Instead, confront your pain and face it as an issue of forgiveness.

Pray to the Lord, "Father, I have been hurt. Please heal my wounded heart. Heal me of these feelings of rejection, alienation, sorrow, and loss."

Confess to the Lord, "I confess that I want to retaliate against this person. I am angry, frustrated, and in pain. I know that these emotions are not going to be helpful to me or resolve the situation. I ask You to forgive me of these negative feelings. I desire to forgive this person, Lord. Help me to forgive."

Then *declare before the Lord with faith*, "I free this person right now from the wrong that he has done against me. I let him go and turn him over to You. You deal with him, Lord. I turn over all responsibility for him to You. Free me from any memories that might haunt me or discourage me in the wake of this hurtful experience. Help me to walk in freedom and strength in relationship to this person and to all others who know of this incident. I trust You to do this, Holy Spirit. And I ask this in Jesus' name. Amen."

The more times you forgive others who hurt you, the more automatic your response will be to forgive. As you forgive and develop a forgiving spirit, you will find that compassion grows in your heart—compassion for those who are sinners, for those who have sinned against you, for those who are struggling with a spirit of unforgiveness. You will find new opportunities to minister to people who are in the bondage of sin, guilt, shame, or unforgiveness.

If you do not forgive immediately and begin to move through the cycle of unforgiveness and forgiveness, you can stop at any stage and move directly to the stage of acknowledging your need to forgive. If you find yourself avoiding God, speaking words of denial, or feeling discouraged, you can go immediately to the Lord and admit your feelings, confess your unforgiveness, make a declaration of forgiveness for the other person, and receive God's healing, forgiveness, and freedom in your life. You can turn to the Lord at any time, and the sooner the better!

> Therefore submit to God. Resist the devil and he will flee from you. Draw near to God and He will draw near to you. Cleanse your hands, you sinners; and purify your hearts, you double-minded. Lament and mourn and weep! Let your laughter be turned to mourning and your joy to gloom. Humble yourselves in the sight of the Lord, and He will lift you up.
>
> —James 4:7–10

≈ In practical terms, how do we "resist the devil"? How is this done in the process of forgiveness?

≈ Give practical examples of how each of the following is done in forgiving another person:

Submit to God:

Draw near to God:

Cleanse your hands:

Purify your hearts:

Lament, mourn, weep:

Humble yourself:

✍ Today and Tomorrow ✍

TODAY: THE CYCLE OF FORGIVENESS IS SHORTENED WHEN I CONFRONT MY
PAIN AND TURN IT OVER TO GOD.

TOMORROW: I WILL TAKE TIME THIS WEEK TO CONFRONT UNRESOLVED
HURTS AND TO FORGIVE THOSE WHO HAVE HURT ME.

LESSON 9

Joseph—A Life of Forgiveness

───────── ❧ **In This Lesson** ❧ ─────────

LEARNING: IS IT REALLY POSSIBLE TO FULLY FORGIVE PEOPLE WHO HAVE
DEEPLY INJURED ME?

GROWING: HOW CAN I MAKE FORGIVENESS PART OF MY CHARACTER, RATH-
ER THAN BITTERNESS?

───────────── ❧ ─────────────

God's Word gives us a great example of a person who embodied a forgiving spirit. That person is Joseph:

> When Joseph's brothers saw that their father was dead, they
> said, "Perhaps Joseph will hate us, and may actually repay us
> for all the evil which we did to him." So they sent messengers
> to Joseph, saying, "Before your father died he commanded,
> saying, 'Thus you shall say to Joseph: "I beg you, please forgive
> the trespass of your brothers and their sin; for they did evil
> to you." ' Now, please, forgive the trespass of the servants of
> the God of your father." And Joseph wept when they spoke to
> him. Then his brothers also went and fell down before his face,
> and they said, "Behold, we are your servants." Joseph said to
> them, "Do not be afraid, for am I in the place of God? But as
> for you, you meant evil against me; but God meant it for good,

in order to bring it about as it is this day, to save many people alive. Now therefore, do not be afraid; I will provide for you and your little ones." And he comforted them and spoke kindly to them.

—Genesis 50:15–21

If any man ever had just cause to be angry with his brothers and to allow a spirit of unforgiveness to develop, it was Joseph. And yet we have no hint in the Scriptures that Joseph ever had an unforgiving spirit.

Consider some of the reasons that Joseph might have had for unforgiveness:

Joseph knew the hatred of his brothers. Joseph had shared with his brothers two prophetic dreams that the Lord had given to him when he was seventeen years old. In one dream, he and his brothers were in a grain field, binding sheaves, and the sheaves of his brothers bowed down to his sheaf. In the second dream, the sun, moon, and eleven stars bowed down to Joseph. The Bible tells us that his brothers "hated him and could not speak peaceably to him." (See Gen. 37:1–10.)

Joseph was misunderstood by his father. Joseph's father, Jacob, rebuked him and said, "What is this dream that you have dreamed? Shall your mother and I and your brothers indeed come to bow down to the earth before you?" Joseph was the eleventh son in a family of twelve sons. He is described as the beloved son. I feel certain that this rebuke from his father wounded him deeply. (See Gen. 37:10.)

Joseph was badly mistreated by his brothers. Joseph's brothers plotted against him and stripped him of his tunic, cast him into a waterless pit, and then sat on the ground above, eating a meal—and no doubt taunting Joseph. They had intended to kill him, but along came a caravan of Midianites, and the brothers decided to sell Joseph into slavery instead. (See Gen. 37:12–28.)

❧ If you had been in Joseph's place, heading into Egypt and slavery, how would you have felt? What would you have thought of your brothers?

❧ What was Joseph's response? (See Genesis 50:15–21, above.)

How do we know that Joseph did not develop an unforgiving spirit in the aftermath of these events? Well, once Joseph was in Egypt, he was purchased by Potiphar, an officer of Pharaoh and the captain of the guard. And we are told that Potiphar "saw that the Lord was with [Joseph] and that the Lord made all he did to prosper in his hand. So Joseph found favor in his sight, and served him. Then he made him overseer of his house, and all that he had he put under his authority" (Gen. 39:3–4).

Had Joseph been a man with an unforgiving spirit, he would have had a seething hatred inside him. Such a spirit eventually manifests itself in some way, usually in acts of rebellion. A person with an unforgiving spirit sometimes has a chip on the shoulder or a surly attitude. A slave with an angry, rebellious attitude is not a person that you put in charge of all your worldly goods. That is not a person that you put in charge of other slaves in your household. That is not a person to whom you entrust your wife and family. Potiphar, however, had complete confidence in Joseph.

Furthermore, Potiphar's estate prospered under Joseph's administration. A person with an unforgiving spirit nearly always seeks to exact some type of revenge—even if not on the person who caused him the original injury. It's a part of the unforgiving person's attempt to regain control, after having felt humiliated and without power. But Joseph didn't act in vengeance against Potiphar. He worked in such a way that Potiphar was blessed.

We know from Joseph's experience in Potiphar's house that he was a forgiving man because of these words: "The Lord blessed the Egyptian's house for Joseph's sake; and the blessing of the Lord was on all that he had in the house and in the field" (Gen. 39:5). God's anointing does not rest on people with an unforgiving spirit.

Joseph was falsely accused by Potiphar's wife. One day Joseph entered Potiphar's house and found himself alone with Potiphar's wife. She attempted to seduce Joseph, but he refused her. She grabbed his outer garment as he attempted to escape her seduction, and he slipped out of his robe and left her holding it. Angry that she was rejected, Potiphar's wife used Joseph's garment as evidence in trumped-up charges of attempted rape, and Potiphar had little recourse other than to commit Joseph to prison. (See Gen. 39:7–20.)

103

How does this illustrate a forgiving spirit in Joseph? A person who has been injured repeatedly in the past, and especially so by those in authority in the immediate family (such as victims of physical and emotional abuse, sexual abuse, or incest) is prone to develop a victim syndrome. A pattern of victimization readily develops unless there is intervention in the person's life to restore a sense of self-esteem. This perception of being a victim often goes hand in glove with unforgiveness. The person relives painful moments, and each time, the memories tear down the person and weaken self-esteem and courage. Ultimately, the person has little inner strength or power to resist the advances of any person who attempts to use or abuse him further, and especially a person who is perceived to be in authority.

Joseph exhibited none of this syndrome. He had no perception of himself as a victim. He operated in strength and conviction in rejecting Potiphar's wife.

> But [Joseph] refused and said to [Potiphar's] wife, "Look, my master does not know what is with me in the house, and he has committed all that he has to my hand. There is no one greater in this house than I, nor has he kept back anything from me but you, because you are his wife. How then can I do this great wickedness, and sin against God?"
>
> —Genesis 39:8–9

∗ What were Joseph's reasons for refusing Potiphar's wife?

🙶 Joseph showed gratitude toward both Potiphar and God. What does this reveal regarding the process of forgiving others?

Joseph was forgotten by a would-be benefactor. In prison, Joseph rose to leadership. The experience with Potiphar's wife did not leave him with a spirit of unforgiveness. Once again, Joseph proved himself worthy of trust. The keeper of the prison turned over all the administration of the prison to Joseph, including supervision of the other prisoners. Again, this is clear evidence that Joseph had not developed an angry, bitter, resentful attitude. (See Gen. 39:21–23.)

In prison, a butler shared a dream with Joseph, which the Lord enabled Joseph to interpret. He told the butler that he would be restored to his position as Pharaoh's cupbearer, and then he said to him,

> Remember me when it is well with you, and please show kindness to me; make mention of me to Pharaoh, and get me out of this house [prison]. For indeed I was stolen away from the land of the Hebrews; and also I have done nothing here that they should put me into the dungeon.
>
> —Genesis 40:14–15

The butler was restored as Joseph foretold, but he neglected to mention Joseph for two full years. Two years is a long time to be forgotten in prison. Bitterness and unforgiveness can take root in that time. How do we know this didn't happen in Joseph's life? Because the day came when the butler remembered Joseph.

Pharaoh had two troubling dreams, and none of his magicians or wise men could interpret them. Joseph was called from prison and brought before Pharaoh. Pharaoh told Joseph his dreams, and with God's help, Joseph interpreted them. Then Joseph gave him God's advice for responding to the situation foretold in the dreams.

A person with an unforgiving spirit usually can't wait to tell the story of his injuries. He is eager to elicit support, sympathy, or justice. Yet Joseph made no appeals on his own behalf at any time in his meeting with Pharaoh. Even when Pharaoh elevated Joseph to a high position in the land of Egypt, Joseph made no request for justice on his own behalf.

It was as if Joseph had completely forgotten all that had happened to him. He had forgiven the failures and sins of others against him, and he moved forward into success in his leadership role. Under Joseph, a plan was put into place that was for the blessing of Egypt and the preservation of people. Joseph was not a man motivated by vengeance.

When have you been forgotten by someone who could have helped you? Did you allow resentment to build toward that person? How did you deal with that resentment?

Facing People Who Hurt Us

The day came when Joseph faced his brothers who had sold him into slavery. They didn't recognize him, but he recognized them. There was no unforgiveness in the way that he dealt with them. In revealing his identity to them, Joseph said,

I am Joseph your brother, whom you sold into Egypt. But now, do not therefore be grieved or angry with yourselves because you sold me here; for God sent me before you to preserve life. For these two years the famine has been in the land, and there are still five years in which there will be neither plowing nor harvesting. And God sent me before you to preserve a posterity for you in the earth, and to save your lives by a great deliverance. So now it was not you who sent me here, but God; and He has made me a father to Pharaoh, and lord of all his house, and a ruler throughout all the land of Egypt. Hurry and go up to my father, and say to him, "Thus says your son Joseph: 'God has made me lord of all Egypt; come down to me, do not tarry. You shall dwell in the land of Goshen, and you shall be near to me, you and your children, your children's children, your flocks and your herds, and all that you have. There I will provide for you, lest you and your household, and all that you have, come to poverty; for there are still five years of famine.' " ... You shall tell my father of all my glory in Egypt, and of all that you have seen; and you shall hurry and bring my father down here. Then he fell on his brother Benjamin's neck and wept, and Benjamin wept on his neck. Moreover he kissed all his brothers and wept over them.

—Genesis 45:4–15

The scene was permeated with forgiveness. The last thing a person with an unforgiving spirit does is seek the good of those who have hurt him. Rather than exact any vengeance or retribution on his brothers, Joseph responded to them with compassion, love, and provision. He wept with them. And above all, he saw God's higher purpose in all the events of his life.

 According to Joseph, how did he arrive in Egypt? Where is his focus in all the events of his life?

 How can this attitude speed the process of forgiving those who betray you?

The Key to a Forgiving Spirit

The key to a forgiving spirit is to see *divine purpose* in any event that happens to you. God has a plan and purpose for your life, and He does not allow adversity to come into your life without a specific reason that eventually can work to your good. Joseph was able to see an ultimate purpose for all that happened to him. He saw God's hand in allowing him to be brought to Egypt. He saw God's hand in giving him experience after experience in which he could grow in leadership skills and understand the ways of the Egyptians. He saw how God protected him and prepared him through the years.

When you can look at any hurtful experience that comes your way and say, "God has a purpose in this," you are on your way to developing a forgiving spirit. God does have a purpose. That purpose may be to do a work in the life of the person who has wronged you. It may be to perfect an area of your life. It may be to make you stronger. It may be to train you to have a forgiving spirit!

Whatever God's reasons may be for you to feel pain or to suffer at the hands of others, the ultimate outcome for you can be good—but only if you are willing to forgive people who hurt you.

How Many Times Are We to Forgive?

We are to forgive continually and immediately, and to forgive all who hurt us. Peter asked Jesus one day, "Lord, how often shall my brother sin against me, and I forgive him? Up to seven times?" (Matt. 18:21). Peter no doubt thought that he was being very generous in citing seven times. But Jesus said to Peter, "I do not say to you, up to seven times, but up to seventy times seven" (Matt. 18:22).

There never comes a time when we can say to an offending person, "You've crossed the line." Our forgiveness is to know no limit.

❧ Has anyone ever injured you 490 times? Have you ever kept a count of injuries?

❧ Have you committed 490 sins in your life? Has the Lord been keeping a count of those sins?

Joseph is an example of repeated forgiveness. He never reached a limit in his ability to forgive others. Neither did Jesus, of course. He extended forgiveness repeatedly during His lifetime. And even as He hung on the cross, He forgave those who had put Him there, saying, "Father, forgive them, for they do not know what they do" (Luke 23:34). We must follow their example.

> Then [Joseph's] brothers also went and fell down before his face, and they said, "Behold, we are your servants." Joseph said to them, "Do not be afraid, for am I in the place of God?

But as for you, you meant evil against me; but God meant it for good, in order to bring it about as it is this day, to save many people alive."

—Genesis 50:18–20

What did Joseph mean when he asked if he was "in the place of God"? What does this suggest about taking revenge?

Why did Joseph forgive his brothers? How did his focus on God's sovereignty help him to forgive?

Today and Tomorrow

TODAY: JOSEPH VIEWED EVERYTHING AS PART OF GOD'S PLAN FOR HIS LIFE, AND THEREFORE COULD FORGIVE OTHERS QUICKLY.

TOMORROW: I WILL ASK THE LORD TO HELP ME SEE HOW HE IS LEADING ALL EVENTS IN MY LIFE.

LESSON 10

The Challenge of Forgiving Ourselves

⟨∾ In This Lesson ∾⟩

LEARNING: BUT WHAT IF I CAN'T FORGIVE MYSELF?

GROWING: HOW CAN I GET OUT FROM UNDER THIS BURDEN OF GUILT AND SHAME?

Sometimes the most difficult person to forgive is the one that you face in the mirror. Forgiveness, however, is not complete until you forgive yourself.

If anybody had reason *not* to forgive himself, it was the apostle Peter. On what must have been the most demanding night of Jesus' life, Peter denied that he knew his Master. Jesus had foretold Peter's behavior, saying, "Before the rooster crows twice, you will deny Me three times." Sure enough, Peter did. (See Mark 14:66–72.)

We don't know how Peter might have cried out to his heavenly Father in the aftermath of what he did that night. We don't know what Peter might have said to the Lord after Jesus' resurrection, but we do know this: Peter trusted Jesus to forgive what he had done. And Jesus trusted Peter to receive forgiveness.

After Jesus rose from the dead, an angel said to the women who came to the tomb, "Go, tell His disciples—and Peter—that He is going before you into Galilee; there you will see Him, as He said to you" (Mark 16:7). Jesus expected Peter to continue to follow Him. And Peter did. Jesus met Peter and some of the disciples by the shore of the Sea of Galilee one morning. Peter heard the Lord's voice calling to him from the shore, and he left his fishing boat and "plunged into the sea"—he was in a hurry to get to Jesus as fast as he could. That is the response of a person who feels fully forgiven.

Jesus asked Peter three times, "Do you love Me?" Three times, Peter said, "Yes, Lord; You know that I love You." Three times, Jesus commanded Peter to care for the lambs and sheep of His flock. At the close of Jesus' conversation with Peter, He said to him the same words that He said at the beginning of their relationship: "Follow Me." (See John 21:1–19.) Peter had a second chance to be Jesus' disciple, and he took the opportunity for full restoration.

Peter became a vigorous leader in the early church in Jerusalem. His sermon on the Feast of Pentecost was one of the most effective and powerful soul-winning sermons ever preached. The text for his sermon was a passage from Joel that ends, "And it shall come to pass that whoever calls on the name of the Lord shall be saved" (Acts 2:21). Peter was also the first to preach the gospel to Gentiles. And what did he say to them? "To Him all the prophets witness that, through His name, whoever believes in Him will receive remission of sins" (Acts 10:43).

Peter never could have preached such sermons or enjoyed such anointing on his life if he had not first been able to receive God's forgiveness for himself. God does not anoint a spirit of unforgiveness, even if the person that you are refusing to forgive is yourself.

Paul's Self-Forgiveness

The apostle Paul also was able to forgive himself. He referred to himself as the "chief" of all sinners (1 Tim. 1:15). That may very well have been the case. It is doubtful that anyone persecuted the early Christian church with more vehemence and zeal than he did. He breathed "threats and murder" against the disciples of Jesus (Acts 9:1).

And yet, nobody preached forgiveness more than Paul. Paul declared, "This is a faithful saying and worthy of all acceptance, that Christ Jesus came into the world to save sinners" (1 Tim. 1:15). No matter what you may have done, you have not "outsinned" Peter and Paul. They received God's *complete* forgiveness, including the ability to forgive themselves—and so can you.

If we are faithless, He remains faithful; He cannot deny Himself.

—2 Timothy 2:13

꙳ When have you been faithless to God? In what way is any sin an act of faithlessness toward God?

꙳ What does it mean that God "cannot deny Himself"? How is it an act of denying God's grace when you won't forgive yourself?

Why Don't We Forgive Ourselves?

We don't forgive ourselves for a number of reasons.

1. We may not have really experienced God's forgiveness. You cannot forgive yourself until you first know in your heart, and accept fully by faith, that God can and does forgive you.

2. We may think that we know something about our sin that God doesn't know—and we assume that God wouldn't forgive us if He knew the full details of our sin. Is there something about the facts, consequences, or motivations of your sin that you believe is hidden from God? Let me assure you, He knows all about what you have done and who you are. The Lord knows your thoughts and motives (1 Cor. 3:20). He sees it all.

3. We are performance-based. We tend to create our self-identities on the basis of things that we have accomplished far more than on the inner qualities that we are developing. Sin is part of our performance, and we feel a need to work very hard to remedy a bad showing and turn our evil deeds into something that can be placed in the "win" column of our lives. God does not forgive us, however, on the basis of our performance. He forgives us because it is His gracious will to forgive.

4. We don't know how to deal with self-disappointment. To be disappointed in people, you must first expect them to do something that they cannot or will not do. God doesn't expect you to go through life without failures and sins. Therefore, God isn't surprised by your failure, and He is not disappointed. God doesn't expect you to come to Him with a report of perfect living, but He does expect you to come to Him in your sin and ask for His forgiveness.

5. We emotionally adjust to the guilt. Some people emotionally adjust themselves to feeling guilty, and they are afraid to be free of their guilt because it has become so much a part of their self-identity. If this describes you, ask God to give you the courage to forgive yourself and live a guilt-free life.

6. We consider ourselves to be exempt or different from other people. Some people think that there are extenuating circumstances of their situation that place them above God's Word. That isn't the case. The Scriptures tell us, "God shows no partiality. But in every nation whoever fears Him and works righteousness is accepted by Him" (Acts 10:34–35). The forgiveness that God gives to one person, He makes available to all.

7. We expect to sin again. Therefore, we reason, we can't forgive ourselves because we know that we are weak and are bound to fail in the future. God knows that, too. Nevertheless, He invites us to come to Him for forgiveness.

8. We are confronted by the consequences of our sin on a regular basis, and we draw a conclusion that we can't be fully forgiven. Sometimes we see the consequences of our sin in someone else's life—perhaps a physical, material, or emotional scar that we have caused. We chastise ourselves each time we see that person struggle, and we feel the weight of our sin once again. Or perhaps that outward sign is in our own lives. For example, we may be in prison for what we have done, so we don't see how we can be forgiven and freed from our sin while the images of bondage are all around us.

Recognize that you are being held captive by more than physical, material, or outward restraints. You are being held captive in your heart. Jesus came to set the captives free. (See Isa. 61:1–2; Luke 4:18.) Don't keep yourself captive when He has given you the keys to your spiritual and psychological prison cell.

9. We have extremely low self-esteem. Some people have such low self-esteem that they can't imagine anything good being done for them. They are reluctant to accept what Jesus did for them, and they have very little ability to do something good for themselves—including forgiving themselves. If you are in this situation, read the many promises of God to you in the Scriptures, and believe them. You are His beloved child.

10. We have a secret fear that we might get away with sin, when we know that we need to be punished. Most of us are raised in homes where we receive punishment of some type for the wrongs we do. We don't feel right if we do something wrong and suffer no consequences for it. Let me assure you, all sin has its consequences. The Lord may or may not ease the consequences of your sin in your life. You may commit a terrible crime, receive God's forgiveness, and still spend many years in prison. You may sin in a way that causes physical damage to your body, receive God's forgiveness, and still suffer in your body. Even if you think that you are getting away with sin, you aren't. It eventually will manifest itself in consequences.

In receiving God's forgiveness and forgiving ourselves, we aren't absolving ourselves of consequences. We are restoring our relationship with our heavenly Father, and we are putting ourselves into a position to receive the help of the Holy Spirit in dealing with the consequences.

There is therefore now no condemnation to those who are in Christ Jesus, who do not walk according to the flesh, but according to the Spirit.

—Romans 8:1

🔖 What does it mean to "walk according to the flesh"? To walk "according to the Spirit"?

🔖 If God has no condemnation for you as His child, what right do you have to condemn yourself? What role are you playing if you do so?

False Guilt

As we discussed in an earlier lesson, there are also times when we find it difficult to forgive ourselves for something, even though we haven't sinned before God. Accidents happen. We fail and make mistakes. Not all errors are sins before God. Not all bad things require God's forgiveness.

For example, consider the case of a man who is driving down the street and a toddler rushes into the street in the path of his car. He isn't speeding. He applies the brakes immediately. Still, his car strikes and seriously injures the child. The man feels great sorrow and remorse, and for years, he is unable to forgive himself for what happened.

This man is suffering false guilt. He has not sinned. He needs to go to God and ask for healing, he needs to ask the Lord to restore his joy, and he needs to accept, by faith, that God will heal him and make him whole. This isn't a matter of sin and forgiveness.

Consider the woman who goes through a divorce that she didn't want. She did everything in her ability to keep her marriage together, but her husband willfully abandons her and her children. She finds it difficult to forgive herself for the divorce and its effects on her children. This woman, too, is suffering false guilt. She has not sinned. She, too, needs to go to God and ask for a healing of her broken heart, and to believe with her faith that God will heal her and renew her ability to love others and to love herself. Hers is not a matter of sin and forgiveness.

~ When have you suffered from false guilt? What effect did it have on your life? On your relationships with others? On your relationship with God?

~ How do you determine whether guilt is false or justified? What role is played by prayer? By wise counsel? By God's Word?

A Failure to Forgive Yourself

A failure to forgive yourself has the same consequences as a failure to forgive others. You will experience emotional bondage, uneasiness in your spirit, and a cloud of uncertainty about your relationship with God. You will find it difficult to relate freely to others, and your ability to minister or witness to others about God's love will be diminished. You may suffer physical damage in your body from the stress of unforgiven sin. You are likely to have your self-respect damaged and your self-esteem diminished. You may develop a false sense of humility. There are no good results from a failure to forgive yourself. There are only negative by-products.

Seven Questions to Ask

If you are struggling with forgiving yourself today, ask yourself these seven questions:

1. Why should I continue to condemn myself when God no longer condemns me? (God has forgiven you; on what basis do you have grounds to override His forgiveness?)

2. Is my self-condemnation drawing me into a more intimate relationship with God? (It cannot.)

3. What good am I doing to myself or others by continually condemning myself? (Nothing good comes from self-condemnation.)

4. Is my unwillingness to forgive myself helping me build healthy, loving relationships? (You may be building relationships, but they cannot be healthy ones.)

5. Is my self-condemnation influencing God? In other words, is God going to be impressed with my lack of self-forgiveness? Is God going to do anything that He would not do if I did forgive myself? (No, on all accounts.)

6. Is there any scriptural basis for continuing to condemn myself? (No. There is scriptural evidence for your not continuing to do so. See Rom. 8:1.)

7. How long do I intend to condemn myself? (How much self-condemnation is enough? How many years of self-unforgiveness suffice?)

The time to forgive yourself is *now*!

The Steps to Self-Forgiveness

The steps to self-forgiveness are the same as those in forgiving others. Make an honest confession of the specific wrongs that you have committed. Admit to God, "I'm guilty." Also confess that you have been harboring unforgiveness against yourself. Confess to God, "I have kept myself in emotional bondage over this. I know it's wrong. I repent of it and ask You to forgive me for doing this to myself."

Then, reaffirm your faith in God's promises of forgiveness. Speak aloud the verses that affirm your salvation. (See 1 John 1:9; John 3:16; Rom. 10:9–10.) Act on your faith and out of your will, saying, "God, on the basis of Your forgiveness of me, I now release myself from all guilt and condemnation. I accept Your forgiveness, and I forgive myself. I declare myself to be *completely* free of this sin, guilt, and shame because of Christ's work in me. Help me to walk with boldness and courage, and to leave all responsibility for this sin behind me at the Cross."

Most assuredly, I say to you, whoever commits sin is a slave of sin. And a slave does not abide in the house forever, but a son abides forever. Therefore if the Son makes you free, you shall be free indeed.

—John 8:34–36

✎ In what ways does God's forgiveness set you free?

✎ How does self-condemnation make you a slave to sin? In what ways is self-condemnation a sin?

My Final Word to You

Our heavenly Father wants you to experience complete forgiveness today:

✎ Forgiveness of your sin nature and all your sins through the atonement of Jesus Christ on the cross

✎ Forgiveness of others

✎ Forgiveness of yourself

Confessing, repenting, and coming to the Father to ask for forgiveness should be as natural and as spontaneous to us as breathing. By doing these things, we maintain our relationship with God and enjoy the many benefits of His intimate presence.

God cannot use you for His purposes on earth if you are harboring sin in your life, or if you are harboring an unforgiving spirit. In His purposes and plans for your life, you will find your purpose, your destiny, your sense of completion and fulfillment, and a sense of abiding satisfaction and wholeness. Don't keep yourself from that blessed state because of your pride, a false sense of humility, false guilt, or unconfessed sin. Acknowledge that you have sinned and that you do sin, and accept His wonderful gift—full forgiveness.

When you receive and experience God's forgiveness, you will be made whole in your humanity, even as you are prepared for ministry in His kingdom and for life everlasting. Choose to experience God's complete forgiveness in your life! You can in this very hour.

> Come to Me, all you who labor and are heavy laden, and I will give you rest.
>
> —Matthew 11:28

What burdens of unforgiveness are weighing you down? What will you do to get free of those burdens?

He has not dealt with us according to our sins, Nor punished us according to our iniquities. For as the heavens are high above the earth, So great is His mercy toward those who fear Him; As far as the east is from the west, So far has He removed our transgressions from us.

—Psalm 103:10–12

How high are "the heavens" above the earth? How great is God's mercy toward you?

If you travel north to south, you will eventually start moving back north again—but this is not possible when traveling east to west. What does this reveal about how far God has removed your sins?

Today and Tomorrow

TODAY: GOD HAS ALREADY FORGIVEN ME, AND I HAVE NO RIGHT TO CONDEMN MYSELF.

TOMORROW: I WILL ASK THE LORD TO SET ME FREE OF MY BURDEN OF GUILT AND SHAME.